CEOE Field 75-76

OPTE
Oklahoma Professional Teaching Examination
Teacher Certification Exam

By: Sharon Wynne, M.S
Southern Connecticut State University

"And, while there's no reason yet to panic, I think it's only prudent that we make preparations to panic."

XAMonline, INC.
Boston

Copyright © 2007 XAMonline, Inc.
All rights reserved. No part of the material protected by this copyright notice may be reproduced or utilized in any form or by any means, electronic or mechanical, including photocopying, recording or by any information storage and retrievable system, without written permission from the copyright holder.

To obtain permission(s) to use the material from this work for any purpose including workshops or seminars, please submit a written request to:

XAMonline, Inc.
21 Orient Ave.
Melrose, MA 02176
Toll Free 1-800-301-4647
Email: info@xamonline.com
Web www.xamonline.com
Fax: 1-781-662-9268

Library of Congress Cataloging-in-Publication Data

Wynne, Sharon A.
 OPTE Oklahoma Professional Teaching Examination Fields 75, 76: Teacher Certification / Sharon A. Wynne. -2nd ed. ISBN 978-1-58197-796-7
 1. OPTE Oklahoma Professional Teaching Examination Fields 75, 76   2. Study Guides.
 3. CEOE   4. Teachers' Certification & Licensure.   5. Careers

Disclaimer:
The opinions expressed in this publication are the sole works of XAMonline and were created independently from the National Education Association, Educational Testing Service, or any State Department of Education, National Evaluation Systems or other testing affiliates.

Between the time of publication and printing, state specific standards as well as testing formats and website information may change that is not included in part or in whole within this product. Sample test questions are developed by XAMonline and reflect similar content as on real tests; however, they are not former tests. XAMonline assembles content that aligns with state standards but makes no claims nor guarantees teacher candidates a passing score. Numerical scores are determined by testing companies such as NES or ETS and then are compared with individual state standards. A passing score varies from state to state.

Printed in the United States of America

CEOE: OPTE Oklahoma Professional Teaching Examination Fields 75, 76
ISBN: 978-1-58197-796-7

TEACHER STUDY GUIDE

Table of Contents

Competencies/Skills   **Page Number**

SUBAREA I—LEARNERS AND THE LEARNING ENVIRONMENT

Competency 001   **The teacher understands how students learn and develop and can provide learning opportunities that support their intellectual, social, and physical development at all grade levels, including early childhood, elementary, middle level, and secondary** 1

    1.1   The teacher understands the processes by which students acquire knowledge and construct meaning 1

    1.2   The teacher understands developmental characteristics of students and how developmental factors affect learning 2

    1.3   The teacher recognizes ways in which a student's development in one domain (e.g., physical, social-emotional, intellectual) may affect other domains 3

    1.4   The teacher applies strategies for promoting learning among students at different developmental levels 4

Competency 002   **The teacher understands that students vary in their approaches to learning and creates instructional opportunities that are adaptable to individual differences of learners** 7

    2.1   The teacher understands differences in students' learning strengths and needs (e.g., related to variations in learning style, multiple intelligences) 7

    2.2   The teacher recognizes and understands factors that may affect learning and performance and adapts instruction to meet the needs of students based on various factors (e.g., family situations, cultural and language differences, socio-economic circumstances, prior learning, special talents, and disabilities) 9

    2.3   The teacher recognizes how to locate and secure resources and support services to meet varied student needs 15

TEACHER STUDY GUIDE

Competency 003   The teacher uses best practices related to motivation and behavior to create learning environments that encourage positive social interaction, self-motivation, and active engagement in learning, thus providing opportunities for success 18

   3.1   The teacher analyzes factors that affect students' motivation to learn (e.g., expectations of parents/guardians and teachers, prior experiences in school) 18

   3.2   The teacher applies instructional strategies that motivate students to learn and achieve (e.g., relating lessons to students' interests, providing opportunities for students to exercise choice in learning) 18

   3.3   The teacher applies principles of effective classroom management (e.g., in relation to appropriate discipline, student decision making, standards of behavior) to establish an atmosphere of cooperation, trust, and mutual support 20

   3.4   The teacher analyzes how aspects of the physical environment (e.g., spatial arrangements, resources, classroom displays) affect learning 23

Competency 004   The teacher understands the process of continuous lifelong learning, the concept of making learning enjoyable, and the need for a willingness to change when the change leads to greater student learning and development 26

   4.1   The teacher encourages students to participate in learning activities that involve intellectual challenge, exploration, and reflection 26

   4.2   The teacher models for students a willingness to consider new ideas or modify behavior in response to new information or changing circumstances 27

   4.3   The teacher designs instructional activities that respond to student initiatives and preferences and that provide opportunities for students to explore topics that are meaningful to them 28

   4.4   The teacher helps students relate classroom learning to their lives outside school and to their personal goals 31

OPTE

TEACHER STUDY GUIDE

SUBAREA II—INSTRUCTION AND ASSESSMENT

Competency 005 **The teacher plans instruction based upon curriculum goals, knowledge of the teaching/learning process, subject matter, students' abilities and differences, and the community, and adapts instruction based upon assessment and reflection** 32

- 5.1 The teacher applies principles and procedures used in instructional planning (e.g., defining lesson or unit objectives, developing lesson plans, choosing appropriate learning activities) 32

- 5.2 The teacher recognizes key factors to consider when planning instruction (e.g., goals, students' characteristics and prior experiences, community characteristics, cultural and ethnic diversity, available time and resources, opportunities for making interdisciplinary connections) 34

- 5.3 The teacher analyzes and revises aspects of a given lesson plan (e.g., organization, approach, activities, comprehensiveness) in response to changing circumstances (e.g., changes in students' interests, opportunities for involvement of parents/guardians/families, availability of resources, current events) 38

- 5.4 The teacher interprets formal and informal assessment results and uses them to plan or modify learning activities 41

- 5.5 The teacher uses a variety of resources (including technology) in planning and implementing instructional activities 42

Competency 006 **The teacher understands curriculum integration processes and uses a variety of instructional strategies to encourage students' development of critical thinking, problem solving, and performance skills and effective use of technology** 44

- 6.1 The teacher understands ways to integrate and implement different curriculum areas to promote student learning 44

- 6.2 The teacher understands principles and techniques associated with specific instructional strategies (e.g., cooperative learning, direct instruction, discovery learning, whole-group discussion, computer-assisted instruction, interdisciplinary instruction) 45

TEACHER STUDY GUIDE

6.3 The teacher applies a variety of instructional approaches to promote the development of higher-order thinking skills and encourage independent learning 48

6.4 The teacher analyzes how various teacher roles (e.g., instructor, facilitator, coach, audience) and student roles (e.g., self-directed learner, group participant, passive observer) may affect learning processes and outcomes 51

6.5 The teacher recognizes ways to enhance learning through the use of print, manipulative, technological, and human resources (e.g., primary documents, unit-counting blocks [Karen], computers and other educational technologies, community experts) 52

Competency 007 The teacher develops knowledge of and uses a variety of effective communication techniques to foster active inquiry, collaboration, and supportive interaction in the classroom 58

7.1 The teacher applies strategies for adapting communication to facilitate student understanding (e.g., providing examples; simplifying complex problems; using visual, aural, and kinesthetic cues) 58

7.2 The teacher fosters students' expressive and receptive communication skills by modeling effective strategies for conveying information, collaborating, questioning, and responding 60

7.3 The teacher interacts with students in ways that demonstrate respect for and sensitivity to individual differences 62

7.4 The teacher understands how to use a variety of communication tools, including computers and other educational technologies, to enrich learning 64

Competency 008 The teacher understands and uses a variety of assessment strategies to evaluate and modify the teaching/learning process ensuring the continuous intellectual, social, and physical development of the learner 66

8.1 The teacher uses assessment to adapt teaching to address the intellectual, social, and physical development of the student 66

8.2	The teacher understands the characteristics and appropriate uses of formal and informal assessments (e.g., criterion and norm-referenced instruments, teacher-designed classroom tests, portfolios, peer assessment, student self-assessment, observation)	68
8.3	The teacher understands measurement principles and assessment concepts (e.g., validity, reliability, bias)	71
8.4	The teacher effectively interprets and communicates assessment results to students, parents/guardians, and colleagues	74

Competency 009   **The teacher shall have an understanding of the importance of assisting students with career awareness and the application of career concepts to the academic curriculum** 78

9.1	The teacher applies strategies to increase students' awareness of connections between academic learning and the workplace (e.g., introducing young children to different types of jobs, integrating authentic learning/work experiences into the curriculum, expanding students' knowledge of career opportunities)	78
9.2	The teacher understands how to involve employers and members of the community in career awareness and preparation activities	79
9.3	The teacher plans and implements learning experiences to address racial, socio-economic, ethnic, and gender stereotyping related to careers	82
9.4	The teacher plans and implements instructional activities that help students develop skills needed in the workplace (e.g., working in teams, problem solving, communication)	82

TEACHER STUDY GUIDE

SUBAREA III—THE PROFESSIONAL ENVIRONMENT

Competency 010   **The teacher evaluates the effects of his/her choices and actions on others (students, parents, and other professionals in the learning community), modifies those actions when needed, and actively seeks opportunities for continued professional growth 84**

    10.1   The teacher applies strategies for self-assessment (e.g., with respect to effectiveness of instruction; relations with colleagues; gender, cultural, and other biases; and interactions with parents/guardians/family members) 84

    10.2   The teacher understands how to evaluate and respond to feedback (e.g., from supervisors, students, parents/guardians, colleagues) 87

    10.3   The teacher utilizes resources to promote professional growth (e.g., colleagues, professional associations, journals) and selects appropriate professional development activities (e.g., in-service training programs, continuing education).. 88

    10.4   The teacher collaborates with other members of the school community (e.g., other teachers, mentors, supervisors, special needs professionals, administrators, support staff) to enhance skills and solve problems... 90

Competency 011   **The teacher understands the State teacher evaluation process, "Oklahoma Criteria for Effective Teaching Performance," and how to incorporate these criteria in designing instructional strategies 91**

    11.1   The teacher understands and incorporates state-mandated standards for teacher performance (e.g., instruction, scheduling, record keeping) 91

    11.2   The teacher recognizes specific practices that meet or fail to meet OCETP standards 91

    11.3   The teacher demonstrates knowledge of OCETP criteria for evaluating teacher skills in managing and delivering instruction ... 92

    11.4   The teacher applies OCETP criteria in reflecting on one's management and instructional practices and determining whether modifications are necessary 93

TEACHER STUDY GUIDE

Competency 012 **The teacher fosters positive interaction with school colleagues, parents/families, and organizations in the community to actively engage them in support of students' learning and well-being** 94

    12.1   The teacher applies strategies for active collaboration with colleagues (e.g., other teachers, mentors, supervisors, special needs professionals, administrators, support staff) to address the needs of students and improve the learning environment 94

    12.2   The teacher understands schools and school systems within the context of the larger community 95

    12.3   The teacher applies strategies for initiating and maintaining effective communication with parents/guardians and recognizing factors that may promote communication in given circumstances 96

    12.4   The teacher recognizes how to use community resources to enrich learning experiences 97

Competency 013 **The teacher understands the legal aspects of teaching, including the rights of students and parents/families, as well as the legal rights and responsibilities of the teacher** 99

    13.1   The teacher applies knowledge of teachers' legal rights and responsibilities (e.g., with regard to student discipline, situations involving suspected child abuse, the expression of political views) 99

    13.2   The teacher understands laws related to students' rights (e.g., assuring equal access to education, providing an appropriate education for students with special needs, maintaining confidentiality, ensuring due process) 101

    13.3   The teacher applies knowledge of the rights and responsibilities of parents/guardians in various situations (e.g., in relation to student records, school attendance) 103

TEACHER STUDY GUIDE

Sample Test 105

Answer Key 123

Multiple Choice Answer Rationale 124

Sample Constructed Response & Rationale 147

Updates to I.D.E.A., 2004 155

TEACHER STUDY GUIDE

Study and Testing Tips

In the preface, emphasis was placed upon the idea of focusing on the right material, in other words, *what* to study in order to prepare for the subject assessments. But equally important is *how* you study.

learning n. 1. the acquiring of knowledge of or skill in (a subject, trade, art, etc.) by study; experience, etc. 2. to come to know (of or about) 3. acquired knowledge or skill. *(Definition courtesy of Webster's New World Dictionary of the American Language, 1987)*

What we call learning is actually a very complicated process built around multi-faceted layers of sensory input and reinforcement. When you were a child, learning largely consisted of trial and error experimentation, (i.e., "Don't touch that," "It's *Hot!*" or "This tastes *Good!*").

But as we grow older and the neurotransmitters within our brain develop, learning takes on deeper, subtler levels. As adults the neural pathways are fully in place, allowing us to make abstract connections, synthesizing all of our previous experiences (which is essentially what knowledge is), into tremendously complicated, cohesive thoughts.

However, you can increase your chances of truly mastering the information by taking some simple, but effective steps.

Study Tips:

1. **<u>Some foods aid the learning process.</u>** Foods such as milk, nuts, seeds, rice, and oats help your study efforts by releasing natural memory enhancers called CCKs (*cholecystokinin*) composed of *tryptophan*, *choline*, and *phenylalanine*. All of these chemicals enhance the neurotransmitters associated with memory. Before studying, try a light, protein-rich meal of eggs, turkey, and fish. All of these foods release the memory enhancing chemicals. The better the connections, the more you comprehend.

    Likewise, before you take a test, stick to a light snack of energy boosting and relaxing foods. A glass of milk, a piece of fruit, or some peanuts all release various memory-boosting chemicals and help you to relax and focus on the subject at hand.

2. **<u>Learn to take great notes.</u>** A by-product of our modern culture is that we have grown accustomed to getting our information in short doses (i.e. TV news sound bites or USA Today style newspaper articles.)

OPTE

Consequently, we've subconsciously trained ourselves to assimilate information better in neat little packages. If your notes are scrawled all over the paper, it fragments the flow of the information. Strive for clarity.

Newspapers use a standard format to achieve clarity. Your notes can be much clearer through use of proper formatting. A very effective format is called the *Cornell Method.* Take a sheet of loose-leaf lined notebook paper and draw a line all the way down the paper about 1-2" from the left-hand edge. Draw another line across the width of the paper about 1-2" up from the bottom. Repeat this process on the reverse side of the page.

Look at the highly effective result. You have ample room for notes, a left hand margin for special emphasis items or inserting supplementary data from the textbook, a large area at the bottom for a brief summary, and a little rectangular space for just about anything you want.

3. **Dissect the material.** Too often we focus on the details and don't gather an understanding of the concept. However, if you simply memorize only dates, places, or names, you may well miss the whole point of the subject.

   A key way to understand things is to put them in your own words. If you are working from a textbook, automatically summarize each paragraph in your mind. If you are outlining text, don't simply copy the author's words. *Rephrase* them in your own words. You remember your own thoughts and words much better than someone else's, and subconsciously tend to associate the important details to the core concepts.

4. **Turn every heading and caption in to a question.** Pull apart written material paragraph by paragraph and don't forget the captions under the illustrations.

   Example: If the heading is "Stream Erosion", flip it around to read "Why do streams erode?" Then answer the questions.

   If you train your mind to think in a series of questions and answers, not only will you learn more, but it also helps to lessen the test anxiety because you are used to answering questions.

5. **Read, Read, Read.** Even if you only have 10 minutes, put your notes or a book in your hand. Your mind is similar to a computer; you have to input data in order to have it processed. *By reading, you are storing data for future retrieval.* The more times you read something, the more you reinforce the storage of data.

Even if you don't fully understand something on the first pass, *your mind stores much of the material for later recall.*

6. **Create the right study atmosphere.** Our bodies respond to an inner clock called biorhythms. Burning the midnight oil works well for some people, but not everyone. If possible, set aside a particular place to study that is free of distractions. Shut off the television, cell phone, pager and exile your friends and family during your study period.

   If you really are bothered by silence, try background music. Not rock, not hip-hop, not country, but classical. Light classical music at a low volume has been shown to aid in concentration. Don't pick anything with lyrics; you end up singing along. Try just about anything by Mozart, generally light and airy, it subconsciously evokes pleasant emotions and helps relax you.

7. **Limit the use of highlighters.** At best, it's difficult to read a page full of yellow, pink, blue, and green streaks. Try staring at a neon sign for a while and you'll soon see my point, the horde of colors obscure the message. A quick note, a brief dash of color, an underline, and an arrow pointing to a particular passage is much clearer than a horde of highlighted words.

8. **Budget your study time.** Although you shouldn't ignore any of the material, allocate your available study time in the same ratio that topics may appear on the test.

TEACHER STUDY GUIDE

Testing Tips:

1. **Don't outsmart yourself.** Don't read anything into the question. Don't make an assumption that the test writer is looking for something else than what is asked. Stick to the question as written and don't read extra things into it.

2. **Read the question and all the choices *twice* before answering the question.** You may miss something by not carefully reading, and then re-reading both the question and the answers. If you really don't have a clue as to the right answer, leave it blank on the first time through. Go on to the other questions, as they may provide a clue as to how to answer the skipped questions. If later on, you still can't answer the skipped ones . . . ***Guess.*** The only penalty for guessing is that you *might* get it wrong. Only one thing is certain; if you don't put anything down, you will get it wrong!

3. **Turn the question into a statement.** Look at the way the questions are worded. The syntax of the question usually provides a clue. Does it seem more familiar as a statement rather than as a question? Does it sound strange? By turning a question into a statement, you may be able to spot if an answer sounds right, and it may also trigger memories of material you have read.

4. **Look for hidden clues**. It's actually very difficult to compose multiple-foil (choice) questions without giving away part of the answer in the options presented. In most multiple-choice questions you can often readily eliminate one or two of the potential answers. This leaves you with only two real possibilities and automatically your odds go to fifty-fifty for very little work.

5. **Trust your instincts.** For every fact that you have read, you subconsciously retain something of that knowledge. On questions that you aren't really certain about, go with your basic instincts, **your first impression on how to answer a question is usually correct.**

6. **Mark your answers directly on the test booklet**. Don't bother trying to fill in the optical scan sheet on the first pass through the test. Just be very careful not to miss-mark your answers when you eventually transcribe them to the scan sheet.

7. **Watch the clock!** You have a set amount of time to answer the questions. Don't get bogged down trying to answer a single question at the expense of 10 questions you can more readily answer.

OPTE

TEACHER STUDY GUIDE

SUBAREA I—LEARNERS AND THE LEARNING ENVIRONMENT

Competency 0001 The teacher understands how students learn and develop and can provide learning opportunities that support their intellectual, social, and physical development at all grade levels, including early childhood, elementary, middle level, and secondary.

Skill 1.1 The teacher understands the processes by which students acquire knowledge and construct meaning.

First, teachers should realize that historically, there are two broad sides regarding the construction of meaning, the application of strategies, etc. One is behavioral learning. Behavioral learning theory suggests that people learn socially or through some sort of stimulation or repetition. For example, when we touch a hot stove, we learn not to do that again. Or, when we make a social error, and are made fun of for it, we learn proper social conventions. Or, we learn to produce something by watching someone do the same thing.

The other broad theory is cognitive. Cognitive learning theories suggest that learning takes place in the mind, and that the mind processes ideas through brain mapping and connections with other material and experiences. In other words, with behaviorism, learning is somewhat external. We see something, for example, and then we copy it. With cognitive theories, learning is internal. For example, we see something, analyze it in our minds, and make sense of it for ourselves. Then, if we choose to copy it, we do, but we do so having internalized (or thought about) the process.

Today, even though behavioral theories exist, most educators believe that children learn cognitively. So, for example, when teachers introduce new topics by relating those topics to information students are already familiar with or exposed to, they are expecting that students will be able to better integrate new information into their memories by attaching it to something that is already there. Or, when teachers apply new learning to real-world situations, they are expecting that the information will make more sense when it is applied to a real situation. In all of the examples given in this standard, the importance is the application of new learning to something concrete. In essence, what is going on with these examples is that the teacher is slowing building on knowledge or adding knowledge to what students already know. Cognitively, this makes a great deal of sense. Think of a file cabinet. When we already have files for certain things, it's easy for us to find a file and throw new information into it. When we're given something that doesn't fit into one of the pre-existing files, we struggle to know what to do with it. The same is true with human minds.

TEACHER STUDY GUIDE

The teacher has a broad knowledge and thorough understanding of the development that typically occurs during the students' current period of life. More importantly, the teacher understands how children learn best during each period of development. The most important premise of child development is that all domains of development (physical, social, and academic) are integrated. Development in each dimension is influenced by the other dimensions. Moreover, today's educator must also have a knowledge of exceptionalities and how these exceptionalities effect all domains of a child's development.

Skill 1.2 The teacher understands developmental characteristics of students and how developmental factors affect learning.

Physical Development

It is important for the teacher to be aware of the physical stage of development and how the child's physical growth and development affect the child's learning. Factors determined by the physical stage of development include: ability to sit and attend, the need for activity, the relationship between physical skills and self-esteem, and the degree to which physical involvement in an activity (as opposed to being able to understand an abstract concept) affects learning.

Cognitive (Academic) Development

Children go through patterns of learning beginning with pre-operational thought processes and move to concrete operational thoughts. Eventually they begin to acquire the mental ability to think about and solve problems in their head because they can manipulate objects symbolically. Children of most ages can use symbols such as words and numbers to represent objects and relations, but they need concrete reference points. It is essential children be encouraged to use and develop the thinking skills that they possess in solving problems that interest them. The content of the curriculum must be relevant, engaging, and meaningful to the students.

Social Development

Children progress through a variety of social stages beginning with an awareness of peers but a lack of concern for their presence. Young children engage in "parallel" activities playing alongside their peers without directly interacting with one another. During the primary years, children develop an intense interest in peers. They establish productive, positive social, and working relationships with one another. This stage of social growth continues to increase in importance throughout the child's school years including intermediate, middle school, and high school years. It is necessary for the teacher to recognize the importance of developing positive peer group relationships and to provide opportunities and support for cooperative small group projects that not only develop cognitive ability but promote peer interaction. The ability to work and relate effectively with peers is of major importance and contributes greatly to the child's sense of competence.

In order to develop this sense of competence, children need to be successful in acquiring the knowledge and skills recognized by our culture as important, especially those skills which promote academic achievement.

Knowledge of age-appropriate expectations is fundamental to the teacher's positive relationship with students and effective instructional strategies. Equally important is the knowledge of what is individually appropriate for the specific children in a classroom. Developmentally oriented teachers approach classroom groups and individual students with a respect for their emerging capabilities. Developmentalists recognize that kids grow in common patterns, but at different rates which usually cannot be accelerated by adult pressure or input. Developmentally oriented teachers know that variance in the school performance of different children often results from differences in their general growth. With the establishment of inclusionary classes throughout the schools, it is vital for all teachers to know the characteristics of students' exceptionalities and their implications on learning.

Skill 1.3 The teacher recognizes ways in which a student's development in one domain (e.g., physical, social-emotional, intellectual) may affect other domains.

Elementary age children face many changes during their early school years, and these changes may positively and/or negatively impact how learning occurs. Some cognitive developments (i.e., learning to read) may broaden their areas of interest as students realize the amount of information (i.e., novels, magazines, non-fiction books) that is out there. On the other hand, a young student's limited comprehension may inhibit some of their confidence (emotional) or conflict with values taught at home (moral). Joke telling (linguistic) becomes popular with children age six or seven, and children may use this newly discovered "talent" to gain friends or social "stature" in their class (social). Learning within one domain often spills over into other areas for young students.

Likewise, learning continues to affect all domains as a child grows. Adolescence is a complex stage of life. While many people joke about the awkwardness of adolescence, it is particularly important to remember that this stage of life is the stage just before adulthood. While people do indeed develop further in adulthood, the changes are not as quick or significant as they are in adolescence.

When we say that development takes place within domains, what we mean is simply that different aspects of a human change. So, for example, physical changes take place (e.g., body growth, sexuality); cognitive changes take place (e.g., better ability to reason); linguistic changes take place (e.g., a child's vocabulary develops further); social changes take place (e.g., figuring out identity); emotional changes take place (e.g., changes in ability to be concerned about other people); and moral changes take place (e.g., testing limits).

TEACHER STUDY GUIDE

The important thing to remember about adolescent development within each of these domains is that they are not exclusive. For example, physical and emotional development are tied intricately, particularly when one feels awkward about his or her body; or when emotional feelings are tied to sexuality; or when one feels that he or she does not look old enough (as rates of growth are obviously not similar). Moral and cognitive development often goes hand in hand when an adolescent reasons behavior or searches for role models.

What do educators need to know about this? Well, first, it is important to be sensitive to changes in adolescents. Just because you see a change in one area does not mean that there aren't bigger changes in another area, hidden beneath the surface. Speaking of which, the second area of extreme importance is to realize that adolescents may be deeply hurt over certain issues that may or may not be directly related to the changes they are going through. It is particularly important for educators to be on the lookout for signs of depression, drug use, and other damaging activities, behaviors, or symptoms.

The educator's primary professional concern will always be for the student and for the development of the student's potential. The educator will therefore strive for professional growth and will seek to exercise the best professional judgment and integrity.

In a student-centered learning environment, the goal is to provide the best education and opportunity for academic success for all students. Integrating the developmental patterns of physical, social and academic norms for students will provide individual learners with student learning plans that are individualized and specific to their skill levels and needs. Teachers who effectively develop and maximize a student's potential will use pre- and post-assessments to gain comprehensive data on the existing skill level of the student in order to plan and adapt curriculum to address and grow student skills. Maintaining communication with the student and parents will provide a community approach to learning where all stakeholders are included to maximize student-learning growth.

Skill 1.4 The teacher applies strategies for promoting learning among students at different developmental levels.

The effective teacher is cognizant of students' individual learning styles and human growth and development theory and applies these principles in the selection and implementation of appropriate instructional activities. In regards to the identification and implementation of appropriate learning activities, effective teachers select and implement instructional activities consistent with principles of human growth and development theory.

Learning activities selected for younger students (below age eight) should focus on short time frames in highly simplified form. The nature of the activity and the content in which the activity is presented affects the approach that the students will take in processing the information. Younger children tend to process information at a slower rate than older children (age eight and older).

On the other hand, when selecting and implementing learning activities for older children, teachers should focus on more complex ideas as older students are capable of understanding more complex instructional activities. Moreover, effective teachers maintain a clear understanding of the developmental appropriateness of activities selected for providing educational instructions to students and select and present these activities in a manner consistent with the level of readiness of his/her students.

The effective teacher takes care to select appropriate activities and classroom situations in which learning is optimized. The classroom teacher should manipulate instructional activities and classroom conditions in a manner that enhances group and individual learning opportunities. For example, the classroom teacher can organize group learning activities in which students are placed in a situation in which cooperation, sharing ideas, and discussion occurs. Cooperative learning activities can assist students in learning to collaborate and share personal and cultural ideas and values in a classroom learning environment.

The effective teacher selects learning activities based on specific learning objectives. Ideally, teachers should not plan activities that fail to augment the specific objectives of the lesson. Learning activities should be planned with a learning objective in mind. Objective driven learning activities tend to serve as a tool to reinforce the teacher's lesson presentation. Additionally, selected learning objectives should be consistent with state and district educational goals that focus on National educational goals (Goals 2000) and the specific strengths and weaknesses of individual students assigned to the teacher's class.

The effective teacher plans his/her learning activities to introduce them in a meaningful instructional sequence. Teachers should combine instructional activities as to reinforce information by providing students with relevant learning experiences through instructional activities.

Differentiating Instruction

Differentiation of instruction means that the teacher will vary the content, process, or product (Tomlinson, 1995). When a teacher varies content, it means that she or he will allow students to learn different things. For example, when studying the American Revolution, students in a social studies class might get a choice on whether they can study battles, daily life in the colonies at the time, or politics. When the teacher varies process, it means that he or she will allow students various ways of completing the same type of work.

TEACHER STUDY GUIDE

For example, some students in a math class may be very proficient with a type of math activity and do not need to work out the problem by hand; other students may need the extra time in order to come to the correct answer. Finally, when teachers vary the product, their students will turn in different things that all show competency in one area. For example, in Language Arts, after reading a book, some students might write a book report, others might complete an art project, and others might do a dramatic interpretation of a section of the book. The reasons for differentiating instruction are based on two important differences in children: interest and ability.

Differentiating reading instruction is a bit more complex. Usually, when a teacher wants to ensure that each student in his or her class is getting the most out of the reading instruction, the teacher will need to consider the level at which the student is proficient in reading—as well as the specific areas that each student struggles with. It is first important to use a variety of sources of data to make decisions on differentiation, rather than rely on just one test, for example.

When teachers have proficient readers in their classrooms, they usually feel that these students need less attention and less work. This is wrong. If these students do not get careful instruction and challenging activities to increase their reading abilities further, they may become disengaged with school. These students benefit greatly from integrating classroom reading with other types of reading, perhaps complementing the whole-class novel with some additional short stories or non-fiction pieces. They also benefit from sustained silent reading, in which they can choose their own books and read independently. Discussion groups and teacher-led discussion activities are also very useful for these students. It is important, however, to ensure that these students do not feel that they have to do extra work than everyone else. Remember, differentiation does not distinguish differences in quantity; it distinguishes differences in type of work.

Average readers may benefit from many of the things that highly proficient readers should do; however, they may need more skill instruction. Most likely, they will not need as much skill instruction as weak readers, but they will benefit highly from having a teacher who knows which skills they are lacking and teaches them to use those skills in their own reading.

Weak readers need to focus highly on skills. Teachers will want to encourage them to make predictions, connect ideas, outline concepts, evaluate, and summarize. The activities that these students engage in should be developed for the purpose of instilling reading strategies that they can use in their independent reading, as well as to propel them toward higher levels of reading.

OPTE

TEACHER STUDY GUIDE

Competency 0002 The teacher understands that students vary in their approaches to learning and creates instructional opportunities that are adaptable to individual differences of learners.

Skill 2.1 The teacher understands differences in students' learning strengths and needs (e.g., related to variations in learning style, multiple intelligences).

There are several educational learning theories that can be applied to classroom practices. One classic learning theory is Piaget's stages of development which consist of four learning stages: sensory motor stage (from birth to age 2); pre-operation stages (ages 2 to 7 or early elementary); concrete operational (ages 7 to 11 or upper elementary); and formal operational (ages 7-15 or late elementary/high school). Piaget believed children passed through this series of stages to develop from the most basic forms of concrete thinking to sophisticated levels of abstract thinking.

Some of the most prominent learning theories in education today include brain-based learning and the Multiple Intelligence Theory. Supported by recent brain research, brain-based learning suggests that knowledge about the way the brain retains information enables educators to design the most effective learning environments. As a results, researchers have developed twelve principles that relate knowledge about the brain to teaching practices. These twelve principles are:

- The brain is a complex adaptive system
- The brain is social
- The search for meaning is innate
- We use patterns to learn more effectively
- Emotions are crucial to developing patterns
- Each brain perceives and creates parts and whole simultaneously
- Learning involves focused and peripheral attention
- Learning involves conscious and unconscious processes
- We have at least two ways of organizing memory
- Learning is developmental
- Complex learning is enhanced by challenged (and inhibited by threat)
- Every brain is unique

(Caine & Caine, 1994, Mind/Brain Learning Principles)

Educators can use these principles to help design methods and environments in their classrooms to maximize student learning.

OPTE

The Multiple Intelligent Theory, developed by Howard Gardner, suggests that students learn in (at least) seven different ways. These include visually/spatially, musically, verbally, logically/mathematically, interpersonally, intrapersonally, and bodily/kinesthetically.

The most current learning theory of constructivist learning allows students to construct learning opportunities. For constructivist teachers, the belief is that students create their own reality of knowledge and how to process and observe the world around them. Students are constantly constructing new ideas, which serve as frameworks for learning and teaching. Researchers have shown that the constructivist model is comprised of the four components:

1. Learner creates knowledge
2. Learner constructs and makes meaningful new knowledge to existing knowledge
3. Learner shapes and constructs knowledge by life experiences and social interactions
4. In constructivist learning communities, the student, teacher and classmates establish knowledge cooperatively on a daily basis.

Kelly (1969) states "human beings construct knowledge systems based on their observations parallels Piaget's theory that individuals construct knowledge systems as they work with others who share a common background of thought and processes." Constructivist learning for students is dynamic and ongoing. For constructivist teachers, the classroom becomes a place where students are encouraged to interact with the instructional process by asking questions and posing new ideas to old theories. The use of cooperative learning that encourages students to work in supportive learning environments using their own ideas to stimulate questions and propose outcomes is a major aspect of a constructivist classroom.

The metacognition learning theory deals with "the study of how to help the learner gain understanding about how knowledge is constructed and about the conscious tools for constructing that knowledge" (Joyce and Weil 1996). The cognitive approach to learning involves the teacher's understanding that teaching the student to process his/her own learning and mastery of skill provides the greatest learning and retention opportunities in the classroom. Students are taught to develop concepts and teach themselves skills in problem solving and critical thinking. The student becomes an active participant in the learning process and the teacher facilitates that conceptual and cognitive learning process.

TEACHER STUDY GUIDE

Social and behavioral theories look at the social interactions of students in the classroom that instruct or impact learning opportunities in the classroom. The psychological approaches behind both theories are subject to individual variables that are learned and applied either proactively or negatively in the classroom. The stimulus of the classroom can promote conducive learning or evoke behavior that is counterproductive for both students and teachers. Students are social beings that normally gravitate to action in the classroom, so teachers must be cognizant in planning classroom environments that provide both focus and engagement in maximizing learning opportunities.

Designing classrooms that provide optimal academic and behavioral support for a diversity of students in the classroom can be daunting for teachers. The ultimate goal for both students and teachers is creating a safe learning environment where students can construct knowledge in an engaging and positive classroom climate of learning.

No one of these theories will work for every classroom, and a good approach is to incorporate a range of learning styles in a classroom. Still, under the guidance of any theory, good educators will differentiate their instructional practices to meet the needs of their students' abilities and interests using various instructional practices.

Skill 2.2 The teacher recognizes and understands factors that may affect learning and performance and adapts instruction to meet the needs of students based on various factors (e.g., family situations, cultural and language differences, socio-economic circumstances, prior learning, special talents, and disabilities).

Oftentimes, students absorb the culture and social environment around them without deciphering contextual meaning of the experiences. When provided with a diversity of cultural contexts, students are able to adapt and incorporate multiple meanings from cultural cues vastly different from their own socioeconomic backgrounds. Socio-cultural factors provide a definitive impact on a students' psychological, emotional, affective, and physiological development, along with a students' academic learning and future opportunities.

The educational experience for most students is a complicated and complex experience with a diversity of interlocking meanings and inferences. If one aspect of the complexity is altered, it affects other aspects, which may impact how a student or teacher views an instructional or learning experience. With the current demographic profile of today's school communities, the complexity of understanding, interpreting, synthesizing the nuances from the diversity of cultural lineages can provide many communication and learning blockages that could impede the acquisition of learning for students.

OPTE

TEACHER STUDY GUIDE

Teachers must create personalized learning communities where every student is a valued member and contributor of the classroom experiences. In classrooms where socio-cultural attributes of the student population are incorporated into the fabric of the learning process, dynamic interrelationships are created that enhance the learning experience and the personalization of learning. When students are provided with numerous academic and social opportunities to share cultural incorporations into the learning, everyone in the classroom benefits from bonding through shared experiences and having an expanded viewpoint of a world experience and culture that vastly differs from their own.

Researchers continue to show that personalized learning environments increase the learning affect for students; decrease drop-out rates among marginalized students; and decrease unproductive student behavior which can result from constant cultural misunderstandings or miscues between students. Promoting diversity of learning and cultural competency in the classroom for students and teachers creates a world of multicultural opportunities and learning. When students are able to step outside their comfort zones and share the world of a homeless student or empathize with an English Language Learner (ELL) student who has just immigrated to the United States and is learning English for the first time and is still trying to keep up with the academic learning in an unfamiliar language; then students grow exponentially in social understanding and cultural connectedness.

Personalized learning communities provide supportive learning environments that address the academic and emotional needs of students. As socio-cultural knowledge is conveyed continuously in the interrelated experiences shared cooperatively and collaboratively in student groupings and individualized learning, the current and future benefits will continue to present the case and importance of understanding the "whole" child, inclusive of the social and the cultural context.

The student's capacity and potential for academic success within the overall educational experience are products of her or his total environment: classroom and school system; home and family; neighborhood and community in general. All of these segments are interrelated and can be supportive, one of the other, or divisive, one against the other. As a matter of course, the teacher will become familiar with all aspects of the system, the school and the classroom pertinent to the students' educational experience. This would include not only process and protocols but also the availability of resources provided to meet the academic, health and welfare needs of students. But it is incumbent upon the teacher to look beyond the boundaries of the school system to identify additional resources as well as issues and situations which will effect (directly or indirectly) a student's ability to succeed in the classroom.

Examples of Resources

- Libraries, museums, zoos, planetariums, etc.
- Clubs, societies and civic organizations, community outreach programs of private businesses and corporations and of government agencies
  These can provide a variety of materials and media as well as possible speakers and presenters
- Departments of social services operating within the local community

These can provide background and program information relevant to social issues which may be impacting individual students. And this can be a resource for classroom instruction regarding life skills, at-risk behaviors, etc.

Initial contacts for resources outside of the school system will usually come from within the system itself: from administration; teacher organizations; department heads; and other colleagues.

Examples of Issues/Situations

- Students from multicultural backgrounds: Curriculum objectives and instructional strategies may be inappropriate and unsuccessful when presented in a single format which relies on the student's understanding and acceptance of the values and common attributes of a specific culture which is not his or her own.

- Parental/family influences: Attitude, resources and encouragement available in the home environment may be attributes for success or failure. Families with higher incomes are able to provide increased opportunities for students. Students from lower income families will need to depend on the resources available from the school system and the community. This should be orchestrated by the classroom teacher in cooperation with school administrators and educational advocates in the community.

Family members with higher levels of education often serve as models for students, and have high expectations for academic success. And families with specific aspirations for children (often, regardless of their own educational background) encourage students to achieve academic success, and are most often active participants in the process.

A family in crisis (caused by economic difficulties, divorce, substance abuse, physical abuse, etc.) creates a negative environment which may profoundly impact all aspects of a student's life, and particularly his or her ability to function academically. The situation may require professional intervention. It is often the classroom teacher who will recognize a family in crisis situation and instigate an intervention by reporting on this to school or civil authorities.

TEACHER STUDY GUIDE

Regardless of the positive or negative impacts on the students' education from outside sources, it is the teacher's responsibility to ensure that all students in the classroom have an equal opportunity for academic success. This begins with the teacher's statement of high expectations for every student, and develops through planning, delivery and evaluation of instruction which provides for inclusion and ensures that all students have equal access to the resources necessary for successful acquisition of the academic skills being taught and measured in the classroom.

Students with Exceptionalities

The term "students with disabilities" never implies one particular type of disability. First, there is significant disagreement over the term "disability," itself. Many people argue that it suggests a defect in a person's character. Regardless, disabilities are often physical; however, many learning disabilities relate to an individual's ability to learn or communicate, for example. While common characteristics cannot easily be applied to all students with disabilities, it is assumed that most disabilities will hamper an individual's ability to perform a specific action. For example, deaf or "hard of hearing" individuals have a difficult time with auditory listening; people with multiple sclerosis may have trouble with muscle function and cannot walk; people with Attention Deficit Hyperactivity Disorder (ADHD) may have trouble concentrating on academic studies. It is important to remember that just because a student has a disability, not all human functions work improperly. In fact, even students with specific disabilities may not be inflicted by all possible symptoms of that particular disability.

How can teachers identify students with disabilities? Well, first remember that students have a right to privacy; often, students who know of a particular disability will not want peers or even teachers to know. Some disabilities necessitate special school care, while others require that parents (and/or doctors) notify school nurses or administrators of specific disabilities. In such cases, teachers often will be notified, yet the teacher should be very cautious about letting that information get out of his/her hands.

Many disabilities may be obvious, particularly those that are physical. In such cases, teachers will notice physical or behavioral abnormalities. Chances are, all of the student's peers have noticed, as well, and it is important to pay attention to teasing or bullying. Quite often, teachers will be informed about a student's disability because of involvement of an Individual Education Plan (IEP). This is brought about as the parent or previous teacher has requested that a student be tested for a particular disability; usually in this case, it is a learning disability.

OPTE

Increasingly, educators have noticed that learning disabilities must be attended to. Such disabilities may include auditory processing disabilities, attention deficit hyperactivity disorder, visual processing disabilities (including varying degrees of blindness), autism, etc. (By the way, autism is a disorder that usually shows up within the first three years of a child's life; it hinders normal communication and social interactive behavior.)

When giftedness is observed, teachers should also concern themselves with ensuring that such children get the attention they need and deserve so that they can continue to learn and grow.

Students Acquiring English

Teaching students who are learning English as a second language poses some unique challenges, particularly in a standards-based environment. The key is realizing that no matter how little English a student knows, the teacher should teach with the student's developmental level in mind. This means that instruction should not be "dumbed-down" for ESOL students. Different approaches should be used, however, to ensure that these students (a) get multiple opportunities to learn and practice English and (b) still learn content.

Many ESOL approaches are based on social learning methods. By being placed in mixed level groups or by being paired with a student of another ability level, students will get a chance to practice English in a natural, non-threatening environment. Students should not be pushed in these groups to use complex language or to experiment with words that are too difficult. They should simply get a chance to practice with simple words and phrases.

In teacher-directed instructional situations, visual aids, such as pictures, objects, and video are particularly effective at helping students make connections between words and items they are already familiar with

ESOL students may need additional accommodations with assessments, assignments, and projects. For example, teachers may find that written tests provide little to no information about a student's understanding of the content. Therefore, an oral test may be better suited for ESOL students. When students are somewhat comfortable and capable with written tests, a shortened test may actually be preferable; take note that they will need extra time to translate.

Adapting Instruction

A positive environment, where open, discussion-oriented, non-threatening communication among all students can occur, is a critical factor in creating an effective learning culture. The teacher must take the lead and model appropriate actions and speech, and intervene quickly when a student makes a misstep and offends (often inadvertently) another.

Communication issues that the teacher in a diverse classroom should be aware of include:

- Be sensitive to terminology and language patterns that may exclude or demean students. Regularly switch between the use of "he" and "she" in speech and writing. Know and use the current terms that ethnic and cultural groups use to identify themselves (e.g., "Latinos" (favored) vs. "Hispanics").
- Be aware of body language that is intimidating or offensive to some cultures, such as direct eye contact, and adjust accordingly.
- Monitor your own reactions to students to ensure equal responses to males and females, as well as differently-performing students.
- Don't "protect" students from criticism because of their ethnicity or gender. Likewise, acknowledge and praise all meritorious work without singling out any one student. Both actions can make all students hyper-aware of ethnic and gender differences and cause anxiety or resentment throughout the class.
- Emphasize the importance of discussing and considering different viewpoints and opinions. Demonstrate and express value for all opinions and comments and lead students to do the same

When teaching in diverse classrooms, teachers must also expect to be working and communicating with all kinds of students. The first obvious difference among students is gender. Interactions with male students are often different than those with female students. Depending on the lesson, female students are more likely to be interested in working with partners or perhaps even individually. On the other hand, male students may enjoy a more collaborative or hands-on activity. The gender of the teacher will also come into play when working with male and female students. Of course, every student is different and may not fit into a stereotypical role, and getting to know their students' preferences for learning will help teachers to truly enhance learning in the classroom.

Most class rosters will consist of students from a variety of cultures, as well. Teachers should get to know their students (of all cultures) so that they may incorporate elements of their cultures into classroom activities and planning. Also, getting to know about a student's background/cultural traditions helps to build a rapport with each student, as well as further educate the teacher about the world in which he or she teaches. See Skill 3.5 for more information about a culturally diverse classroom.

TEACHER STUDY GUIDE

For students still learning English, teachers must make every attempt to communicate with that student daily. Whether it's with another student who speaks the same language, word cards, computer programs, drawings or other methods, teachers must find ways to encourage each student's participation. Of course, the teacher must also be sure the appropriate language services begin for the student in a timely manner, as well.

Teachers must also consider students from various socioeconomic backgrounds. These students are just as likely as anyone else to work well in a classroom; unfortunately, sometimes difficulties occur with these children when it comes to completing homework consistently. These students may need help deriving a homework system or perhaps need more attention on study or test-taking skills. Teachers should encourage these students as much as possible and offer positive reinforcements when they meet or exceed classroom expectations. Teachers should also watch these students carefully for signs of malnutrition, fatigue and possibly learning disorders.

Skill 2.3 The teacher recognizes how to locate and secure resources and support services to meet varied student needs.

A teacher's responsibility to students extends beyond the four walls of the school building. In addition to offering well-planned and articulately delivered lessons, the teacher must consider the effects of both body language and spoken language on students' learning. Furthermore, today's educator must address the needs of diverse learners within a single classroom. The teacher is able to attain materials that may be necessary for the majority of the regular education students and some of the special needs children and, more and more frequently, one individual student. The "effective" teacher knows that there are currently hundreds of adaptive materials that could be used to help these students increase achievement and develop skills.

Student-centered classrooms contain not only textbooks, workbooks, and literature materials but also rely heavily on a variety of audio-visual equipment and computers. There are tape recorders, language masters, filmstrip projectors, and laser disc players to help meet the learning styles of the students.

Although most school centers cannot supply all the materials that special needs students require, each district more than likely has a resource center where teachers can check out special equipment. Most communities support agencies which offer assistance in providing the necessities of special needs people including students. Teachers must know how to obtain a wide range of materials including school supplies, medical care, clothing, food, adaptive computers and books (such as Braille), eye glasses, hearing aids, wheelchairs, counseling, transportation, etc.

TEACHER STUDY GUIDE

Individuals with Disabilities
Collaborative teams play a crucial role in meeting the needs of all students, and they are important step to identifying students with special needs. Under the Individuals with Disabilities Act (IDEA), which federally mandates special education services in every state, it is the responsibility of public schools to ensure consultative, evaluative and if necessary, prescriptive services to children with special needs. In most school districts, this responsibility is handled by a collaborative group called the Child Study Team (CST). If a teacher or parent suspects a child to have academic, social or emotional problems are referred to the CST where a team consisting of educational professionals (including teachers, specialists, the school psychologist, guidance, and other support staff) review the student's case and situation through meetings with the teacher and/or parents/guardians. The CST will determine what evaluations or tests are necessary, if any, and will also assess the results. Based on these results, the CST will suggest a plan of action if one is felt necessary.

Inclusion, mainstreaming, and least restrictive environment
Inclusion, mainstreaming and least restrictive environment are interrelated policies under the IDEA, with varying degrees of statutory imperatives.
- Inclusion is the right of students with disabilities to be placed in the regular classroom
- Least restrictive environment is the mandate that children be educated to the maximum extent appropriate with their non-disabled peers
- Mainstreaming is a policy where disabled students can be placed in the regular classroom, as long as such placement does not interfere with the student's educational plan

One plan of action is an Academic Intervention Plan (AIP). An AIP consists of additional instructional services that are provided to the student in order to help them better achieve academically if the student has met certain criteria (such as scoring below the state reference point on standardized tests or performing more than two levels below grade-level).

Another plan of action is a 504 plan. A 504 plan is a legal document based on the provisions of the Rehabilitation Act of 1973 (which preceded IDEA). A 504 plan is a plan for instructional services to assist students with special needs in a regular education classroom setting. When a student's physical, emotional, or other impairments (such as Attention Deficit Disorder) impact his or her ability to learn in a regular education classroom setting, that student can be referred for a 504 meeting. Typically, the CST and perhaps even the student's physician or therapist will participate in the 504 meeting and review to determine in a 504 plan will be written.

TEACHER STUDY GUIDE

Finally, a child referred to CST may qualify for an Individualized Education Plan (IEP). An IEP is a legal document which delineates the specific, adapted services a student with disabilities will receive. An IEP differs from a 504 plan in that the child must be identified for special education services to qualify for an IEP, and ALL students who receive special education services must have an IEP. Each IEP must contain statements pertaining to the student's present performance level, annual goals, related services and supplementary aids, testing modifications, a projected date of services, and assessment methods for monitoring progress. Each year, the CST and guardians must meet to review and update a student's IEP.

TEACHER STUDY GUIDE

Competency 0003 The teacher uses best practices related to motivation and behavior to create learning environments that encourage positive social interaction, self-motivation, and active engagement in learning, thus providing opportunities for success.

Skill 3.1 The teacher analyzes factors that affect students' motivation to learn (e.g., expectations of parents/guardians and teachers, prior experiences in school).

Teachers need to be aware that much of what they say and do can be motivating and may have a positive effect on students' achievement. Studies have been conducted to determine the impact of teacher behavior on student performance. Surprisingly, a teacher's voice can really make an impression on students. Teachers' voices have several dimensions—volume, pitch, rate, etc. A recent study on the effects of speech rate indicates that, although both boys and girls prefer to listen at the rate of about 200 words per minute, boys tend to prefer slower rates overall than girls. This same study indicates that a slower rate of speech directly affects processing ability and comprehension.

Other speech factors such as communication of ideas, communication of emotion, distinctness/pronunciation, quality variation and phrasing, correlate with teaching criterion scores. These scores show that "good" teachers ("good" meaning teachers who positively impact and motivate students) use more variety in speech than do "less effective" teachers. A teacher's speech skills can be strong motivating elements. A teacher's body language has an even greater effect on student achievement and ability to set and focus on goals. Teacher smiles provide support and give feedback about the teacher's affective state. A deadpan expression can actually be a detriment to the student's progress. Teacher frowns are perceived by students to mean displeasure, disapproval, and even anger. Studies also show that teacher posture and movement are indicators of the teacher's enthusiasm and energy, which emphatically influence student learning, attitudes, motivation, and focus on goals. Teachers have a greater efficacy on student motivation than any person other than parents.

Skill 3.2 The teacher applies instructional strategies that motivate students to learn and achieve (e.g., relating lessons to students' interests, providing opportunities for students to exercise choice in learning).

If a teacher can help students to take responsibility for their own ideas and thoughts, much has been accomplished. They will only reach that level in a non-judgmental environment, an environment that doesn't permit criticism of the ideas of others and that accepts any topic for discussion that is in the realm of appropriateness. Success in problem solving boosts students' confidence and makes them more willing to take risks, and the teacher must provide those opportunities for success.

OPTE

Develop success-oriented activities

Success-oriented activities are tasks that are selected to meet the individual needs of the student. During the time a student is learning a new skill, tasks should be selected so that the student will be able to earn a high percentage of correct answers during the teacher questioning and seatwork portions of the lesson. Later, the teacher should also include work that challenges students to apply what they have learned and stimulate their thinking.

Skill knowledge, strategy use, motivation, and personal interests are all factors that influence individual student success. The student who can't be bothered with reading the classroom textbook may be highly motivated to read the driver's handbook for his or her license, or the rulebook for the latest video game. Students who did not master their multiplication tables will likely have problems working with fractions.

In the success-oriented classroom, mistakes are viewed as a natural part of the learning process. The teacher can also show that adults make mistakes by correcting errors without getting unduly upset. The students feel safe to try new things because they know that they have a supportive environment and can correct their mistakes.

Activities that promote student success:
   a) are based on useful, relevant content that is clearly specified, and organized for easy learning
   b) allow sufficient time to learn the skill and is selected for high rate of success
   c) allow students the opportunity to work independently, self-monitor, and set goals
   d) provide for frequent monitoring and corrective feedback
   e) include collaboration in group activities or peer teaching

Students with learning problems often attribute their successes to luck or ease of the task. Their failures are often blamed on their supposed lack of ability, difficulty of the task, or the fault of someone else. Successful activities, attribution retraining, and learning strategies can help these students to discover that they can become independent learners. When the teacher communicates the expectation that the students can be successful learners and chooses activities that will help them be successful, achievement is increased.

Skill 3.3 The teacher applies principles of effective classroom management (e.g., in relation to appropriate discipline, student decision making, standards of behavior) to establish an atmosphere of cooperation, trust, and mutual support.

Classroom management plans should be in place when the school year begins. Developing a management plan takes a proactive approach—that is, decide what behaviors will be expected of the class as a whole, anticipate possible problems, and teach the behaviors early in the school year, and behavior management techniques should focus on positive procedures that can be used at home as well at school. Involving the students in the development of the classroom rules lets the students know the rationale for the rules, allows them to assume responsibility in the rules because they had a part in developing them. When students get involved in helping establish the rules, they will be more likely to assume responsibility for following them. Once the rules are established, enforcement and reinforcement for following the rules should begin right away.

Consequences should be introduced when the rules are introduced, clearly stated, and understood by all of the students. The severity of the consequence should match the severity of the offense and must be enforceable. The teacher must apply the consequence consistently and fairly; so the students will know what to expect when they choose to break a rule.

Like consequences, students should understand what rewards to expect for following the rules. The teacher should never promise a reward that cannot be delivered, and follow through with the reward as soon as possible. Consistency and fairness is also necessary for rewards to be effective. Students will become frustrated and give up if they see that rewards and consequences are not delivered timely and fairly.

About four to six classroom rules should be posted where students can easily see and read them. These rules should be stated positively, and describe specific behaviors so they are easy to understand. Certain rules may also be tailored to meet target goals and IEP requirements of individual students. (For example, a new student who has had problems with leaving the classroom may need an individual behavior contract to assist him or her with adjusting to the class rule about remaining in the assigned area.) As the students demonstrate the behaviors, the teacher should provide reinforcement and corrective feedback. Periodic "refresher" practice can be done as needed, for example, after a long holiday or if students begin to "slack off." A copy of the classroom plan should be readily available for substitute use, and the classroom aide should also be familiar with the plan and procedures.

TEACHER STUDY GUIDE

The teacher should clarify and model the expected behavior for the students. In addition to the classroom management plan, a management plan should be developed for special situations, (i.e., fire drills) and transitions (i.e., going to and from the cafeteria). Periodic review of the rules, as well as modeling and practice, may be conducted as needed, such as after an extended school holiday.

Procedures that use social humiliation, withholding of basic needs, pain, or extreme discomfort should never be used in a behavior management plan. Emergency intervention procedures used when the student is a danger to himself or others are not considered behavior management procedures. Throughout the year, the teacher should periodically review the types of interventions being used, assess the effectiveness of the interventions used in the management plan, and make revisions as needed for the best interests of the child.

Deviant behavior can lead to more off-task time than any other factor in today's classrooms. Effective teachers reduce the incidence of these behaviors through clear-cut rules and consistency. If the teacher is consistent, then the students know what to expect, and learn very quickly that they, too, must be consistent. Beginning-teacher programs teach that effective teachers state the rules, explain the rules, and then put the students through a guided practice of the rules. This results in a clear understanding of what behaviors are expected in the classroom from each student. Moreover, it is more efficient to reduce the occurrence of deviant behaviors rather than to have to deal with them happening. Effective teachers achieve this through clear-cut rule explication and consistent monitoring.

Furthermore, effective teachers maintain a business-like atmosphere in the classroom. This leads to the students getting on-task quickly when instruction begins. There are many ways effective teachers begin instruction immediately. One method is through the use of over-head projectors. The teacher turns-on the overhead the second class begins, and the students begin taking notes. The teacher is then free to circulate for the first few minutes of class and settle-down individual students as necessary. Additionally, having a routine that is followed regularly at the beginning of class allows the students to begin without waiting for teacher instruction. Therefore, effective teachers maintain business-like consistent classrooms.

In conclusion, effective teachers utilize an efficient use of class time. The teacher understands it is important to begin class promptly because of the enormous amount of teaching time that can be lost. Therefore, effective teachers attend to attendance procedures, and other non-academic tasks routinely while maintaining on-task behavior among the students.

TEACHER STUDY GUIDE

Behavior Management Plan Strategies for Increasing Desired Behaviors

1. Prompt

A prompt is a visual or verbal cue that assists the child through the behavior shaping process. In some cases, the teacher may use a physical prompt such as guiding a child's hand. Visual cues include signs or other visual aids. Verbal cues include talking a child through the steps of a task. The gradual removal of the prompt as the child masters the target behavior is called fading.

1. Modeling

In order for modeling to be effective, the child must first be at a cognitive and developmental level to imitate the model. Teachers are behavior models in the classroom, but peers are powerful models as well, especially in adolescence. A child who does not perceive a model as acceptable will not likely copy the model's behavior. This is why teachers should be careful to reinforce appropriate behavior and not fall into the trap of attending to inappropriate behaviors. Children who see that the students who misbehave get the teacher's constant attention will most likely begin to model those students' behaviors.

2. Contingency Contracting

Also known as the Premack Principle or "Grandma's Law", this technique is based on the concept that a preferred behavior that frequently occurs can be used to increase a less preferred behavior with a low rate of occurrence. In short, performance of X results in the opportunity to do Y, such as getting 10 minutes of free time for completing the math assignment with 85% accuracy.

Contingency contracts are a process that continues after formal schooling and into the world of work and adult living. Contracts can be individualized, developed with input of the child, and accent positive behaviors. Contingencies can also be simple verbal contracts, such as the teacher telling a child that he or she may earn a treat or special activity for completion of a specific academic activity. Contingency contracts can be simple daily contracts or more formal, written contracts.

Written contracts last for longer periods of time, and must be clear, specific, and fair. Payoffs should be deliverable immediately after the student completes the terms of the contract. An advantage of a written contract is that the child can see and re-affirm the terms of the contract. By being actively involved in the development of the contract with the teacher and/or parent, the child assumes responsibility for fulfilling his share of the deal. Contracts can be renewed and renegotiated as the student progresses toward the target behavior goal.

OPTE

4. Token Economy

A token economy mirrors our money system in that the students earn tokens ("money") which are of little value in themselves, but can be traded for tangible or activity rewards, just as currency can be spent for merchandise. Using stamps, stickers, stars, or point cards instead of items like poker chips decrease the likelihood of theft, loss, and noise in the classroom.

Tips for a token economy:

a) keep the system simple to understand and administer
b) develop a reward "menu" which is deliverable and varied
c) decide on the target behaviors
d) explain the system completely and in positive terms before beginning the economy
e) periodically review the rules
f) price the rewards and costs fairly, and post the menu where it will be easily read
g) gradually fade to a variable schedule of reinforcement

Skill 3.4 The teacher analyzes how aspects of the physical environment (e.g., spatial arrangements, resources, classroom displays) affect learning.

The physical setting of the classroom contributes a great deal toward the propensity for students to learn. An adequate, well-built, and well-equipped classroom will invite students to learn. This has been called "invitational learning." Among the important factors to consider in the physical setting of the classroom are the following:

a) adequate physical space
b) repair status
c) lighting adequacy
d) adequate entry/exit access (including handicap accessibility)
e) ventilation/climate control
f) coloration

A classroom must have adequate physical space so students can conduct themselves comfortably. Some students are distracted by windows, pencil sharpeners, doors, etc. Some students prefer the front, middle, or back rows.

The teacher has the responsibility to report any items of classroom disrepair to maintenance staff. Broken windows, falling plaster, exposed sharp surfaces, leaks in ceiling or walls, and other items of disrepair present hazards to students.

Another factor which must be considered is adequate lighting. Report any inadequacies in classroom illumination. Florescent lights placed at acute angles often burn out faster. A healthy supply of spare tubes is a sound investment.

Local fire and safety codes dictate entry and exit standards. In addition, all corridors and classrooms should be wheelchair accessible for students and others who use them. Older schools may not have this accessibility.

Another consideration is adequate ventilation and climate control. Some classrooms in some states use air conditioning extensively. Sometimes it is so cold as to be considered a distraction. Specialty classes such as science require specialized hoods for ventilation. Physical Education classes have the added responsibility for shower areas and specialized environments that must be heated such as pool or athletic training rooms.

Classrooms with warmer subdued colors contribute to students' concentration on task items. Neutral hues for coloration of walls, ceiling, and carpet or tile are generally used in classrooms so distraction due to classroom coloration may be minimized.

In the modern classroom, there is a great deal of furniture, equipment, supplies, appliances, and learning aids to help the teacher teach and students learn. The classroom should be provided with furnishings that fit the purpose of the classroom. The kindergarten classroom may have a reading center, a playhouse, a puzzle table, student work desks/tables, a sandbox, and any other relevant learning/interest areas.

Whatever the arrangement of furniture and equipment may be the teacher must provide for adequate traffic flow. Rows of desks must have adequate space between them for students to move and for the teacher to circulate. All areas must be open to line-of-sight supervision by the teacher.

In all cases, proper care must be taken to ensure student safety. Furniture and equipment should be situated safely at all times. No equipment, materials, boxes, etc. should be placed where there is danger of falling over. Doors must have entry and exit accessibility at all times.

Instructional momentum requires an organized system for material placement and distribution. Inability to find an overhead transparency, a necessary chart page, or the handout worksheet for the day not only stops the momentum, but is very irritating to students. Materials not appearing in an expected classroom site frustrates both teacher and students. Major categories on performance measurement system instruments are "Handles materials well" and "Maintains instructional momentum."

In the lower grades an organized system uses a "classroom helper" for effective distribution and collection of books, equipment, supplies, etc. The classroom helpers should be taught to replace the materials in the proper places to obtain them easily for the next time they are used. Periodically, the teacher should inspect to see that all materials are in the proper places and are ready for use as needed.

At higher grade levels, the teacher is concerned with materials such as textbooks, written instructional aids, worksheets, computer programs, etc., which must be produced, maintained, distributed, and collected for future use. One important consideration is the production of sufficient copies of duplicated materials to satisfy classroom needs. Another is the efficient distribution of worksheets and other materials. The teacher may decide to hand out materials as students are in their learning sites (desks, etc.), or to have distribution materials at a clearly specified place (or small number of places) in the classroom. In any case, there should be firmly established procedures, completely understood by student for receiving classroom materials. Special fields such as physical education or media specialists are well schooled in these areas.

Competency 0004 The teacher understands the process of continuous lifelong learning, the concept of making learning enjoyable, and the need for a willingness to change when the change leads to greater student learning and development.

Skill 4.1 The teacher encourages students to participate in learning activities that involve intellectual challenge, exploration, and reflection.

Teachers can enhance student motivation by planning and directing interactive, "hands-on" learning experiences. Research substantiates that cooperative group projects decrease student behavior problems and increase student on-task behavior. Students who are directly involved with learning activities are more motivated to complete a task to the best of their ability.

The effective teacher takes care as to select appropriate activities and classroom situations in which learning is optimized. The classroom teacher should manipulate instructional activities and classroom conditions in a manner that enhances group and individual learning opportunities. For example, the classroom teacher can organize group learning activities in which students are placed in a situation in which cooperation, sharing ideas, and discussion occurs. Cooperative learning activities can assist students in learning to collaborate and share personal and cultural ideas and values in a classroom learning environment.

Teachers who couple diversity in instructional practices with engaging and challenging curriculum and the latest advances in technology can create the ultimate learning environment for creative thinking and continuous learning for students. Teachers who are innovative and creative in instructional practices are able to model and foster creative thinking in their students. Encouraging students to maintain journals and portfolios of their valued work from projects and assignments will allow students to make conscious choices on including a diversity of their creative endeavors in a filing format that can be treasured throughout the educational journey.

The ability to create a personal and professional charting of student's academic and emotional growth found within the performance-based assessment of individualized portfolios becomes a toolkit for both students and teachers. Teachers can use semester portfolios to gauge student academic progress and personal growth of students who are constantly changing their self-images and worldviews on a daily basis. When a student is studying to master a math concept and is able to create visual of the learnings that transcend beyond the initial concept to create a bridge connecting a higher level of thinking and application of knowledge, then the teacher can share a moment of enjoyable math comprehension with the student.

The idea of using art concepts as visual imagery in helping students process conceptual learning of reading, math and science skills creates a mental mind mapping of learning for students processing new information. Using graphic organizers and concept web guides that center around a concept and the applications of the concept is an instructional strategy that teachers can use to guide students into further inquiry of the subject matter. Imagine the research of the German chemist Fredrich August Kekule when he looked into a fire one night and solved the molecular structure of benzene and you can imagine fostering that same creativity in students. Helping students understand the art of "visualization" and the creativity of discovery may impart a student visualizing the cure for AIDS or Cancer or how to create reading programs for the next generation of readers.

Skill 4.2 The teacher models for students a willingness to consider new ideas or modify behavior in response to new information or changing circumstances

While the views of knowledge as fixed or objective and fluid or subjective seem to be at odds, most contemporary educators have found a middle ground.

Let's take this apart. First, the view that knowledge is fixed and objective suggests that everything in the world has a truth to it. While we may not be able to know the truth of everything (for example, the number of stars in the solar system), this view suggests that it is *possible* to know the truth about everything. On the other hand, the view that knowledge is subjective fits within a constructivist model of learning that suggests that truths are interpreted differently be different people.

Most readers will see that neither side is perfect. Teachers in particular realize that while there are essential truths, people may have different interpretations *about* those truths. In other words, each student in a classroom will construct a different viewpoint about the curriculum. Often, the different viewpoints come from students' personal backgrounds, including their life experiences, their families, and their religions.

In addition to various viewpoints, often, knowledge changes as time progresses. Things that were true a few years ago may have been adapted and modified based on new information. For example, approximately ten years ago, coffee was seen as a minor threat to human health. Then, new medical research demonstrated that coffee had health benefits. Then, even more medical research suggested that coffee had some benefits and some detriments to health. Now, medical research shows that the health benefits of coffee outweigh the minor negative aspects of coffee. All this goes to show that what we learn as fact one day can be altered greatly the next.

How does this apply to teaching? While facts must and should be taught in various circumstances, factual knowledge is not necessarily the foundation of a strong education. Because facts change rapidly, and because factual information is endless, students often have greater long-term success when they are taught skills to find, evaluate, and utilize facts in a variety of contexts. Concepts built on facts are often more valuable that simple facts lacking a meaningful context, but even then, multiple interpretations can be given to most concepts.

How can teachers model an adaptability to the differing views of truths and the progression of knowledge? Teachers can connect all student learning to essential questions. In other words, while a lesson or unit might focus on the Civil War, teachers can ensure that students know WHY they are learning about the Civil War. Perhaps the teacher wants to help build a strong foundation of the roots of our country. Perhaps the teacher also wants to give students the skills to conduct research through encyclopedias and websites. And perhaps the teacher wants the students to analyze historical events based on their causes and effects. All of these components of learning suggest that information is fluid and subjective in some regard, but that getting the known facts straight is also important for a shared language among all learners.

Finally, teachers can demonstrate to students that multiple interpretations are valued. Students do indeed need to be taught how to offer an educated opinion and to support it. Likewise, they need to be taught how to accept another person's viewpoint, even if it differs from their own.

Skill 4.3 The teacher designs instructional activities that respond to student initiatives and preferences and that provide opportunities for students to explore topics that are meaningful to them

When students are interested in the lesson, their interest and motivation for learning increases. Teachers should provide opportunities so students may work toward becoming self-directed, and therefore, self-motivated, learners.

Skill knowledge, strategy use, motivation, and personal interests are all factors that influence individual student success. Success-oriented activities are tasks that are selected to meet the individual needs and interests of the student. During the time a student is learning a new skill, tasks should be selected so that the student will be able to earn a high percentage of correct answers during the teacher questioning and seatwork portions of the lesson. Later, the teacher should also include work that challenges students to apply what they have learned and stimulate their thinking.

TEACHER STUDY GUIDE

In the success-oriented classroom, mistakes are viewed as a natural part of the learning process. The teacher can also show that adults make mistakes by correcting errors without getting unduly upset. The students feel safe to try new things because they know that they have a supportive environment and can correct their mistakes.

Activities that promote student success:
- f) are based on useful, relevant content that is clearly specified, and organized for easy learning
- g) allow sufficient time to learn the skill and is selected for high rate of success
- h) allow students the opportunity to work independently, self-monitor, and set goals
- i) provide for frequent monitoring and corrective feedback
- j) include collaboration in group activities or peer teaching

Students with learning problems often attribute their successes to luck or ease of the task. Their failures are often blamed on their supposed lack of ability, difficulty of the task, or the fault of someone else. Successful activities, attribution retraining, and learning strategies can help these students to discover that they can become independent learners. When the teacher communicates the expectation that the students can be successful learners and chooses activities that will help them be successful, achievement is increased.

TEACHER STUDY GUIDE

Develop a plan for progression from directed to self-directed activity

Learning progresses in stages from initial acquisition, when the student needs a lot of teacher guidance and instruction to adaptation, when the student can apply what he or she has learned to new situations outside the classroom. As students progress through the stages of learning, the teacher gradually decreases the amount of direct instruction and guidance and encourages the student to function independently. The ultimate goal of the learning process is to teach students how to be independent and apply their knowledge. A summary of these states and their features appears here:

State	Teacher Activity	Emphasis
Initial Acquisition	Provide rationale Guidance Demonstration Modeling Shaping Cueing	Errorless learning Backward Chaining (working from the final product backward through the steps) Forward Chaining (proceeding through the steps to a final product)
Advanced Acquisition	Feedback Error correction Specific directions	Criterion evaluation Reinforcement and reward for accuracy
Proficiency	Positive reinforcement Progress monitoring Teach self-management Increased teacher expectations	Increase speed or performance to the automatic level with accuracy Set goals Self-management
Maintenance	Withdraw direct reinforcement Retention and memory Over learning Intermittent schedule of reinforcement	Maintain high level of performance Mnemonic techniques Social and intrinsic reinforcement
Generalization	Corrective feedback	Perform skill in different times and places
Adaptation	Stress independent problem-solving	Independent problem-solving methods No direct guidance or direct instruction

OPTE

TEACHER STUDY GUIDE

Skill 4.4 The teacher helps students relate classroom learning to their lives outside school and to their personal goals.

Students' attitudes and perceptions about learning are the most powerful factors influencing academic focus and success. When instructional objectives center on students' interests and are relevant to their lives, effective learning occurs. Learners must believe that the tasks that they are asked to perform have some value and that they have the ability and resources to perform them. If a student thinks a task is unimportant, he/she will not put much effort into it. If a student thinks he lacks the ability or resources to successfully complete a task, even attempting the task becomes too great a risk. Not only must the teacher understand the students' abilities and interests, she must also help students develop positive attitudes and perceptions about tasks and learning.

Teachers should have a toolkit of instructional strategies, materials and technologies to encourage and teach students how to problem solve and think critically about subject content. With each curriculum chosen by a district for school implementation, comes an expectation that students must master benchmarks and standards of learning skills. There is an established level of academic performance and proficiency in public schools that students are required to master in today's classrooms. Research of national and state standards indicate that there are additional benchmarks and learning objectives in the subject areas of science, foreign language, English language arts, history, art, health, civics, economics, geography, physical education, mathematics, and social studies that students are required to master in state assessments (Marzano & Kendall, 1996).

Students use basic skills to understand things that are read such as a reading passage or a math word problem or directions for a project. However, students apply additional thinking skills to fully comprehend how what was read could be applied to their own life or how to make comparatives or choices based on the factual information given. These higher-order thinking skills are called critical thinking skills as students think about thinking and teachers are instrumental in helping students use these skills in everyday activities:

- Analyzing bills for overcharges
- Comparing shopping ads or catalogue deals
- Finding the main idea from readings
- Applying what's been learned to new situations
- Gathering information/data from a diversity of sources to plan a project
- Following a sequence of directions
- Looking for cause and effect relationships
- Comparing and contrasting information in synthesizing information

Attention to learner needs during planning is foremost and includes identification of that which the students already know or need to know; the matching of learner needs with instructional elements such as content, materials, activities, and goals; and the determination of whether or not students have performed at an acceptable level, following instruction.

OPTE

TEACHER STUDY GUIDE

SUBAREA II—INSTRUCTION AND ASSESSMENT

Competency 0005 The teacher plans instruction based upon curriculum goals, knowledge of the teaching/learning process, subject matter, students' abilities and differences, and the community, and adapts instruction based upon assessment and reflection.

Skill 5.1 The teacher applies principles and procedures used in instructional planning (e.g., defining lesson or unit objectives, developing lesson plans, choosing appropriate learning activities).

Teaching was once seen as developing lesson plans, teaching, going home early and taking the summer off. However, the demands of a classroom involve much more than grading papers. To begin with, just writing lesson plans is very complicated. Lesson plans are important in guiding instruction in the classroom. Incorporating the nuts and bolts of a teaching unit, the lesson plan outlines the steps of teacher implementation and assessment of teacher instructional capacity and student learning capacity. Teachers are able to objectify and quantify learning goals and targets in terms of incorporating effective performance-based assessments and projected criteria for identifying when a student has learned the material presented.

All components of a lesson plan including the unit description, learning targets, learning experiences, explanation of learning rationale and assessments must be present to provide both quantifiable and qualitative data to ascertain whether student learning has taken place and whether effective teaching has occurred for the students. National and state learning standards must be taken into account because not only will she and her students be measured by the students' scores at the end of the year, the school will also. So, not only must the teacher be knowledgeable about state and local standards, she must structure her own classes in ways that will meet those frameworks.

On the large scale, the teacher must think about the scope of her ambitious plans for the day, the week, the unit, the semester, the year. The teacher must decide on the subject matter for the unit, semester, year, making certain that it is appropriate to the age of the students, relevant to their real lives, and in their realm of anticipated interest. Should she introduce politically controversial issues or avoid them? She must make these decisions deliberatively on the basis of feedback from her students, at the same time keeping sight of her objectives.

TEACHER STUDY GUIDE

The teacher must be very knowledgeable about the writing of behavioral objectives that fall within the guidelines of the state and local expectations, and her objectives must be measurable so that when the unit or semester is complete, she can know for sure whether she has accomplished what she set out to do. Once long range goals have been identified and established, it is important to ensure that all goals and objectives are in conjunction with student ability and needs. Some objectives may be too basic for a higher level student, while others cannot be met with a student's current level of knowledge. There are many forms of evaluating student needs to ensure that all goals set are challenging yet achievable.

Teachers should check a student's cumulative file, located in guidance, for reading level and prior subject area achievement. This provides a basis for goal setting but shouldn't be the only method used. Depending on the subject area, basic skills test, reading level evaluations, writing samples, and/or interest surveys can all be useful in determining if all goals are appropriate. Informal observation should always be used as well. Finally, it is important to take into consideration the student's level of motivation when addressing student needs.

When given objectives by the school or county, teachers may wish to adapt them so that they can meet the needs of their student population. For example, if a high level advanced class is given the objective, "*State five causes of World War II,*" a teacher may wish to adapt the objective to a higher level. "*State five causes of World War II and explain how they contributed to the start of the war.*" Subsequently objectives can be modified for a lower level as well. "*From a list of causes, pick three that specifically caused World War II.*"

When organizing and sequencing objectives, remember that skills are building blocks. A taxonomy of educational objectives can be helpful to construct all organize objectives. Knowledge of material is low on a taxonomy and should be worked with early in the sequence. For example, memorizing definitions or memorizing famous quotes. Eventually, objectives should be developed to include higher level thinking such as comprehension (i.e., being able to use a definition); application (i.e., being able to apply the definition to other situations); synthesis (i.e., being able to add other information); and evaluation (i.e., being able to judge the value of something).

Emergent curriculum describes the projects and themes that classrooms embark on that have been inspired by the children's interests. The teacher uses all the tools of assessment available to her to know as much as she can about her students, and then she continually assesses them over the period of the unit or semester. As she gets to know them, she listens to what their interests are and creates a curriculum in response to what she learns from her observations of her own students.

TEACHER STUDY GUIDE

Skill 5.2 The teacher recognizes key factors to consider when planning instruction (e.g., goals, students' characteristics and prior experiences, community characteristics, cultural and ethnic diversity, available time and resources, opportunities for making interdisciplinary connections).

Effective planning is a key component of effective teaching. Planning is used to select the content and methods that will aid students in mastering set learning objectives. Some of the key elements that must be considered when planning instruction include the following:

Goals

The first step in planning successful instruction is knowing what students will be held accountable for. While teachers may have the best of intentions in teaching numerous, exciting topics, there are only so many days in a school year. The teacher must be aware of what educational objectives must be met by the students and have a set of criteria to indicate when these specific goals are met. Goals are general statements that describe what the teacher intends to accomplish in a lesson. Objectives are more specific and describe what students will be able to do in order to demonstrate the new learning that has occurred as a result of the lesson or unit.

Furthermore, the more content is "covered" (skimmed over, so that students can be exposed to everything), the less students will have deep and lasting understandings of content. So, with that in mind, teachers will benefit from laying out all crucial standards throughout the year and aligning them in a fashion that allows for conceptual growth. Conceptual growth refers to concepts building upon one another. Certain topics simply should be taught before other topics.

Once long range goals have been identified and established, it is important to ensure that all goals and objectives are in conjunction with student ability and needs. Some objectives may be too basic for a higher level student, while others cannot be met with a student's current level of knowledge. There are many forms of evaluating student needs to ensure that all goals set are challenging yet achievable.

Teachers should check a student's cumulative file, located in guidance, for reading level and prior subject area achievement. This provides a basis for goal setting but shouldn't be the only method used. Depending on the subject area, basic skills test, reading level evaluations, writing samples, and/or interest surveys can all be useful in determining if all goals are appropriate. Informal observation should always be used as well. Finally, it is important to take into consideration the student's level of motivation when addressing student needs.

OPTE

TEACHER STUDY GUIDE

When given objectives by the school or county, teachers may wish to adapt them so that they can meet the needs of their student population. For example, if a high level advanced class is given the objective, "*State five causes of World War II,*" a teacher may wish to adapt the objective to a higher level. "*State five causes of World War II and explain how they contributed to the start of the war.*" Subsequently objectives can be modified for a lower level as well. "*From a list of causes, pick three that specifically caused World War II.*"

Next, teachers should consider how students will be required to demonstrate proficiency of the various concepts. This is important, as all instruction should focus on making sure that students can indeed demonstrate proficiency.

Prior Experiences

Students and their needs, including developmental and readiness levels as well as prior knowledge, must be taken into account. The teacher must be aware of the background of the individual students. Their prior experiences in the educational setting should also be taken into account. This should include their family background, their previous grades, test scores, strengths, weaknesses, and how their previous teacher's viewed them. Determining student needs is complicated by the fact that nearly all classrooms include a wide variety of developmental and ability levels as well as students with special needs.

To determine the abilities of incoming students, it may be helpful to consult their prior academic records. Letter grades assigned at previous levels of instruction as well as scores on standardized tests may be taken into account. In addition, the teacher may choose to administer pre-tests at the beginning of the school year, and perhaps also at the initial stage of each new unit of instruction. The textbooks available for classroom use may provide suitable pre-tests, tests of student progress, and post-tests.

In selecting tests and other assessment tools, the teacher should keep in mind that different kinds of tests measure different aspects of student development. The tests included in most textbooks chosen for the classroom, and in the teacher's book that accompanies them are usually achievement tests. Few of these are the type of tests intended to measure the students' inherent ability or aptitude. Teachers will find it difficult to raise students' scores on ability tests, but students' scores on achievement tests may be expected to improve with proper instruction and application in the area being studied.

In addition to administering tests, the teacher may assess the readiness of students for a particular level of instruction by having them demonstrate their ability to perform some relevant task. In a class that emphasizes written composition, for example, students may be asked to submit writing samples. These may be used not only to assure the placement of the students into the proper level, but as a diagnostic tool to help them understand what aspects of their composition skills may need improvement. In the like manner, students in a speech class may be asked to make an impromptu oral presentation before beginning a new level or specific level of instruction. Others may be asked to demonstrate their psychomotor skills in a physical education class, display their computational skills in a mathematics class, and so on. Whatever the chosen task, the teacher will need to select or devise an appropriate assessment scale and interpret the results with care.

Readiness

The concept of readiness is generally regarded as a developmentally based phenomenon. Various abilities, whether cognitive, affective, or psychomotor, are perceived to be dependent upon the mastery or development of certain prerequisite skills or abilities. Readiness, then, implies that the necessary prior knowledge, experience, and readiness prerequisites should not engage in the new task until first acquiring the necessary readiness foundation.

However, at each grade level, there exist readiness expectations and assumptions based on the previous year's instruction. Students who have not yet mastered those concepts are not ready to progress. Failure on the part of the teacher to address student deficiencies may lead to failure of the student to learn the new material.

Readiness for subject area learning is dependent not only on prior knowledge, but also on affective factors such as interest, motivation, and attitude. These factors are often more influential on student learning than the pre-existing cognitive base. It should be noted, then, that a concept such as "readiness to learn" is too broad to be meaningful. Readiness needs to be considered in terms of readiness to "learn science" or, even more accurately, readiness to "learn photosynthesis." Since it is not feasible for the classroom teacher to assess each student's readiness for each lesson, mastery of one lesson is generally assumed to imply readiness for the next sequential lesson.

TEACHER STUDY GUIDE

Diversity

The racial, cultural, and ethnic breakdown of the community that students come from should be taken into account when planning lessons that will be directly applicable to a student in respective communities. In addition, cultural, ethnic, and economic diversity are also factors that influence content decisions. The teacher must ensure that different cultural and ethnic groups are addressed in the class especially when setting curriculum themes, topics, and subjects and how they are addressed. They must ensure that the themes are not culturally or ethnically insensitive or that certain cultures or left out of the lesson who may be a dominant or insignificant part of the class.

Planning Instruction

Once the teacher has a firm handle on his or her students' overall readiness, the teacher will know how and when to pre-teach concepts, what vocabulary skills are needed (i.e., before beginning a class novel or textbook chapter), and how to adjust instruction to meet the needs and interests of all the students.

Lesson plans should include a rationale that explains why a specific lesson is necessary or important. A rationale helps to justify the need for teaching a topic or content to both the student and the parent's. This enables the student to see how the topic is relevant to them and helps to motivate the student.

When organizing and sequencing objectives, remember that skills are building blocks. A taxonomy of educational objectives can be helpful to construct all organize objectives. Knowledge of material is low on a taxonomy and should be worked with early in the sequence. For example, memorizing definitions or memorizing famous quotes. Eventually, objectives should be developed to include higher level thinking such as comprehension (i.e., being able to use a definition); application (i.e., being able to apply the definition to other situations); synthesis (i.e., being able to add other information); and evaluation (i.e., being able to judge the value of something).

Diverse Learners

Social and behavioral theories look at the social interactions of students in the classroom that instruct or impact learning opportunities in the classroom. The psychological approaches behind both theories are subject to individual variables that are learned and applied either proactively or negatively in the classroom. The stimulus of the classroom can promote conducive learning or evoke behavior that is counterproductive for both students and teachers. Students are social beings that normally gravitate to action in the classroom, so teachers must be cognizant in planning classroom environments that provide both focus and engagement in maximizing learning opportunities.

OPTE

Designing classrooms that provide optimal academic and behavioral support for a diversity of students in the classroom can be daunting for teachers. The ultimate goal for both students and teachers is creating a safe learning environment where students can construct knowledge in an engaging and positive classroom climate of learning.

Time Resources

As lessons and units are planned, to be most efficient with time, teachers should determine how much students already understand and how long the concept will take to fully teach. This will allow the teacher to develop lessons that build on students' background knowledge without repeating it. It will also help teachers manage getting in so many standards in a one year time period.

The school calendar and time constraints are factors that should be taken into account during planning. There is not enough time for all the different things that teachers need to do. It is important to establish priorities, about unit content and determine which topics to include, which to emphasize, and which to leave out. When planning instruction teachers must take into account the amount of time available to teach a particular unit of instruction. They must ensure that the lesson can be completely understood and learned in the time allotted and make room for occasions when re-teaching or teaching in another style must take place when the majority of the class does not comprehend the lesson. The availability of resources and materials is a significant aspect as this can often limit the range of possibilities for instructional activities. The Internet can be used to locate resources that can be utilized in lesson planning.

Skill 5.3 The teacher analyzes and revises aspects of a given lesson plan (e.g., organization, approach, activities, comprehensiveness) in response to changing circumstances (e.g., changes in students' interests, opportunities for involvement of parents/guardians/families, availability of resources, current events).

Lesson plans are important in guiding instruction in the classroom. Incorporating the nuts and bolts of a teaching unit, the lesson plan outlines the steps of teacher implementation and assessment of teacher instructional capacity and student learning capacity. Teachers are able to objectify and quantify learning goals and targets in terms of incorporating effective performance-based assessments and projected criteria for identifying when a student has learned the material presented. All components of a lesson plan including the unit description, learning targets, learning experiences, explanation of learning rationale and assessments must be present to provide both quantifiable and qualitative data to ascertain whether student learning has taken place and whether effective teaching has occurred for the students.

TEACHER STUDY GUIDE

A typical format would include the following items below:
1. Written instructional lesson plan-guidelines for what is being taught and how the students will be able to access the information. Subsequent evaluations and assessments will determine whether students have learned or correctly processed the subject content being taught.
2. Unit Description-provides description of the learning and classroom environment.
    a. Classroom Characteristics-describe the physical arrangements of the classroom, along with the student grouping patterns for the lesson being taught. Classroom rules and consequences should be clearly posted and visible.
    b. Student Characteristics-demographics of the classroom that includes student number, gender, cultural and ethnic backgrounds, along with Independent Education students with IEPs (Individualized Education Plans).
3. Learning Goals/Targets/Objectives-what are the expectations of the lessons. Are the learning goals appropriate to the state learning standards and District academic goals? Are the targets appropriate for the grade level, subject content area and inclusive of a multicultural perspective and global viewpoint.
4. Learning Experiences for students-How will student learning be supported using the learning goals?
    a. What prior knowledge or experiences will the students bring to the lesson? How will you check and verify that student knowledge?
    b. How will you engage all students in the classroom? How will students who have been identified as marginalized in the classroom be engaged in the lesson unit?
    c. How will the lesson plan be modified for students with IEPs and how will Independent Education students be evaluated for learning and processing of the modified lesson targets?
    d. How will the multicultural aspect be incorporated into the lesson plan?
    e. What interdisciplinary linkages and connections will be used to incorporate across other subject areas.
    f. What types of assessments/evaluations will be used to test student understanding and processing of the lesson plan?
    g. How will students be cooperatively grouped to engage in the lesson?
    h. What Internet linkages are provided in the lesson plan?
5. Rationales for Learning Experiences-provide data on how the lesson plan addresses student learning goals and objectives. Address whether the lesson provides accommodations for students with IEPs and provides support for marginalized students in the classroom.

6. Assessments-constructing pre and post assessments that evaluate student learning as it correlates to the learning goals and objectives. Do the assessments include a cultural integration that address the cultural needs and inclusion of students.

Flexibility and Instruction

Teachers will also change instructional strategies based on the questions and verbal comments of the students. If the students express confusion or doubt or are unclear in any way about the content of the lesson, the teacher will immediately take another approach in presenting the lesson. Sometimes this can be accomplished by simply rephrasing an explanation. At other times, it will be necessary for the teacher to use visual organizers or models for understanding to be clear. Effective teachers are sensitive to the reactions and responses of their students and will almost intuitively know when instruction is valid and when it is not. Teachers will constantly check for student comprehension, attention, and focus throughout the presentation of a lesson.

After the teacher has presented a skill or concept lesson she will allow time for the students to practice the skill or concept. At this point it is essential for the teacher to circulate among the students to check for understanding. If the teacher observes that any of the students did not clearly understand the skill or concept, then she must immediately readdress the issue using another technique or approach.

A teacher's ultimate goal is ensuring that students learn. And because student learning depends on many factors, including the engagement students have in a lesson, specific "teachable" moments, and other issues that arise in the learning environment, it is important that teachers pay close attention for things that might reduce optimal learning. While assessment is thought of as an official or structured activity (such as a test or an assignment), teachers can also begin to think of assessment as unofficial, informal, and ongoing, as well.

Here's an example: Let's say that a science teacher has prepared a lesson on a very difficult science concept. Knowing that the concept is not simple, the teacher develops a lesson that she believes is very engaging. However, half-way through the lesson, the teacher notices that students are either puzzled or bored. Realizing that continuing the lesson "as is" will not promote deep learning, the teacher immediately changes the situation and alters the lesson to promote better engagement and understanding.

Or, let's say that the science teacher notices that a particular student question draws great interest among other students. The question is sparked by the content, related to science, but not part of the teacher's learning objective. That teacher would be irresponsible to just move forward and ignore the question. To ignore it would be to say to students that learning is supposed to be boring and that school is not supposed to feed the intellectual interests of students. Assessing a sense of curiosity in the students, the teacher engages students in a brief answer to the question.

Let's say the science teacher incorporated a brief experiment as a learning exercise for her particular learning objectives in that lesson. Walking around watching students, she notices that students are making incorrect attributions to the things they are finding in their experiments. The science teacher pauses the experiment and re-teaches a simple concept. Students can then proceed to finish the experiment.

These examples demonstrate how an expert teacher adjusts lessons to meet the learning needs of students on an on-going basis. It proves that any well-planned lesson still may need adjustment. It also shows that the good teacher should look out for ways to make a good lesson better—even if it's in the middle of the lesson delivery!

Skill 5.4 The teacher interprets formal and informal assessment results and uses them to plan or modify learning activities.

The information contained within student records, teacher observations and diagnostic tests are only as valuable as the teacher's ability to understand it. Although the student's cumulative record will contain this information, it is the responsibility of each teacher to read and interpret the information. Diagnostic test results are somewhat uniform and easy to interpret. They usually include a scoring guide that tells the teacher what the numbers actually mean. Teachers also need to realize that these number scores leave room for uncontrollable factor and are not the ultimate indicator of a child's ability or learning needs. Many factors influence these scores including the rapport the child had with the tester, how the child was feeling when the test was administered, and how the child regarded the value or importance of the test. Therefore, the teacher should regard these scores as a "ball park" figure.

When a teacher reads another teacher's observations, it is important to keep in mind that each person brings to an observation certain biases. The reader may also influence the information contained within an observation with his/her own interpretation. When using teacher observations as a basis for designing learning programs, it is necessary to be aware of these shortcomings.

Student records may provide the most assistance in guiding instruction. These records contain information that was gathered over a period of time and may show student growth and progress. They also contain information provided by several people including teachers, parents, and other educational professionals. By reading this compilation of information the teacher may get a more accurate "feel for" a student's needs. All of this information is only a stepping-stone in determining how a child learns, what a child knows, and what a child needs to know to further his/her education.

Skill 5.5 The teacher uses a variety of resources (including technology) in planning and implementing instructional activities.

If we have learned anything in education over the last few decades, it is that students do not all learn in the same way. Furthermore, we have learned that a steady diet of lecture and textbook reading is an extremely ineffective method of instruction. While students definitely should be exposed to lecture and textbooks, they will greatly benefit with the creativity and ingenuity of teachers who find outside resources to assist in the presentation of new knowledge.

Let's first discuss some possibilities: textual and media references, hands-on materials, and technology. Lately, some people have referred to the concept of "multiple texts" as a method of bringing into the classroom multiple types of texts. For example, a social studies teacher might ask students to read an historical novel to complement a unit of study. In addition to texts, appropriately selected video or audio recordings may be useful. For example, a science teacher may wish to show a short clip of a video that demonstrates how to conduct a particular experiment before students do it on their own. Or, a Language Arts teacher may bring in an audio recording of a book to present a uniquely dramatized reading of the book.

Hands-on materials are very important to student learning. For example, math teachers may introduce geometric principles with quilt blocks. The very idea of a science experiment is that hands-on materials and activities more quickly convey scientific ideas to students than do lectures and textbooks.

Finally, technologies, such as personal computers, are very important for student learning. First, it is extremely important that students learn new technologies so that they can easily adapt to the myriad of uses found in business and industry. Second, technology can provide knowledge resources that go beyond what a school library, for example, may be able to offer. Students will need increasingly to learn how to search for, evaluate, and utilize appropriate information in the internet.

TEACHER STUDY GUIDE

Choosing an appropriate reference, text, material, or technology depends on many factors. First, realize that whatever is brought into the class should be done so based on the knowledge that the item will assist students in learning academic standards. There is no reason for any teacher, for example, to show a movie to his or her students that is not for the explicit purpose of helping students reach specific academic objectives, tied to the curriculum. Second, consider the developmental level of the students you are working with. You would not want to introduce complex experiments to second graders; likewise, you would not want to assume that twelfth graders have no knowledge of the internet.

TEACHER STUDY GUIDE

Competency 0006 The teacher understands curriculum integration processes and uses a variety of instructional strategies to encourage students' development of critical thinking, problem solving, and performance skills and effective use of technology.

Skill 6.1 The teacher understands ways to integrate and implement different curriculum areas to promote student learning.

Educators have viewed curriculum integration and interdisciplinary teaching with increasing interest as the educational system continues to search for ways improve student learning and performance. Competence, or even mastery, in one subject area is no longer sufficient to succeed in school, or later, in the workplace. No matter one's area of concentration, a person must be able to: communicate effectively with others, both verbally and in writing; use critical thinking to problem-solve creatively and efficiently; understand numbers and their relationships; and, identify and extend connections between concepts and situations.

The effective teacher seeks to connect, where possible and sensible, their core subject with other subject matter in lessons and assignments. Such connections often involve the development of real-life applications of information, which students can more easily absorb and relate to their previous knowledge and experiences. A language arts unit lesson covering a novel about the Wild West may feature a brief introduction or discussion of the history of the settlement of the West, along with information about geography (using maps and other graphical aids), climate, living conditions, populations, and other facts that ground and enhance the reading and critical analysis experience.

Teachers can incorporate interdisciplinary techniques into their everyday lessons to accomplish cross-curricular teaching:
- Present a combination of subjects, with an emphasis on projects that allow for a broader objective scope;
- Use sources beyond textbooks (e.g., newspapers, the Internet, brochures);
- Show and establish relationships among concepts;
- Use thematic, rather than subject-focused, units as organizing principles;
- Use flexible student groupings to promote a diversity of experience.

A fully developed interdisciplinary teaching effort requires the participation of a teaching team, consisting of faculty representing each of the core disciplines and a curriculum advisor. The team plans the curricula jointly and develops content themes, each of which is taught simultaneously across the core subjects (and where possible, across all subjects). One such theme may be mountains, for example, and the disciplines of literature, math, geography, geology, history and art present interconnected units incorporating this theme.

Skill 6.2 The teacher understands principles and techniques associated with specific instructional strategies (e.g., cooperative learning, direct instruction, discovery learning, whole-group discussion, computer-assisted instruction, interdisciplinary instruction)

Discovery Learning

Beginning at birth, discovery learning is a normal part of the growing-up experience, and this naturally occurring phenomenon can be used to improve the outcomes in your classrooms. Discovery learning in the classroom is based upon inquiry. It has been a factor in all the advances mankind has made through the years. For example, Rousseau constantly questioned his world, particularly the philosophies and theories that were commonly accepted. Dewey, himself a great discoverer, wrote, "There is an intimate and necessary relation between the processes of actual experience and education." Piaget, Bruner, and Papert have all recommended this teaching method. In discovery learning, students solve problems by using their own experience and prior knowledge to determine what truths can be learned. Bruner wrote "Emphasis on discovery in learning has precisely the effect on the learner of leading him to a constructionist, to organize what he is encountering in a manner not only designed to discover regularity and relatedness, but also to avoid the kind of information drift that fails to keep account of the uses to which information might have to be put."

Whole Group Discussion

Whole group discussion can be used in a variety of settings, but the most common is in the discussion of an assignment. Since learning is peer-based with this strategy, students gain a different perspective on the topic, as well as learn to respect the ideas of others. One obstacle that can occur with this teaching method is that the same people tend to participate over and over and the same people do not participate time after time. However, with proper teacher guidance during this activity, whole group discussions are highly valuable.

Case Method Learning

Providing an opportunity for students to apply what they learn in the classroom to real-life experiences has proven to be an effective way of both disseminating and integrating knowledge. The case method is an instructional strategy that engages students in active discussion about issues and problems inherent in practical application. It can highlight fundamental dilemmas or critical issues and provide a format for role playing ambiguous or controversial scenarios. Obviously, a successful class discussion involves planning on the part of the instructor and preparation on the part of the students. Instructors should communicate this commitment to the students on the first day of class by clearly articulating course expectations. Just as the instructor carefully plans the learning experience, the students must comprehend the assigned reading and show up for class on time, ready to learn.

TEACHER STUDY GUIDE

Inquiry

All learning begins with the learner. What children know and what they want to learn are not just constraints on what can be taught; they are the very foundation for learning. Dewey's description of the four primary interests of the child are still appropriate starting points:
1. the child's instinctive desire to find things out
2. in conversation, the propensity children have to communicate
3. in construction, their delight in making things
4. in their gifts of artistic expression.

Questioning

Questioning is a teaching strategy as old as Socrates. The important thing for the teacher to remember is that it must be deliberative and carefully planned. This is an important tool for leading students into critical thinking.

Play

There are so many useful games available that the most difficult task is choosing which will fit into your classroom. Some are electronic, some are board games, and some are designed to be played by a child individually. Even in those cases, a review of the results by the entire classroom can be a useful learning experience.

Learning centers

In a flexible classroom where students have some time when they can choose which activity they will participate in, learning centers are extremely important. They take out-of-class time for creating them, collecting the items that will make them up, and then setting up the center. In some classes, the students might participate in creating a learning center.

Small group work

In the diverse classrooms we are responsible for nowadays, small group work is vital. Children can be grouped according to their level of development or the small groups themselves can be diverse, giving the students who are struggling an opportunity to learn from a student who is already proficient. The better prepared student will learn from becoming a source for the weaker student, and the weaker student may be more likely to accept help from another student sometimes than from the teacher.

Revisiting

Revisiting should occur during a unit, at the end of a unit, and at the end of a semester. In other words, giving students more than one opportunity to grasp principles and skills and to integrate them is practical teaching theory.

TEACHER STUDY GUIDE

Reflection

Teaching can move along so rapidly sometimes that students fail to incorporate what they've learned and to think about it in terms of what they bring to the topic in the first place. Providing time for reflection and guiding students in developing tools for it is a wise teaching method.

Projects

Seeing a unit as a project is also very useful. It opens the door naturally to a multi-task approach to learning. Not only will the students learn about birds, they will have an opportunity to observe them, they can try their hands at drawing them, and they can learn to differentiate one from the other. It's easy to see how a lifetime interest in bird watching can take root in such a project, which is more effective than in simply reading about the topic and talking about it.

Cooperative Learning

Cooperative learning situations, as practiced in today's classrooms, grew out of searches conducted by several groups in the early 1970's. Cooperative learning situations can range from very formal applications such as STAD (Student Teams-Achievement Divisions) and CIRC (Cooperative Integrated Reading and Composition) to less formal groupings known variously as "group investigation," "learning together," "discovery groups." Cooperative learning as a general term is now firmly recognized and established as a teaching and learning technique in American schools.

Since cooperative learning techniques are so widely diffused in the schools, it is necessary to orient students in the skills by which cooperative learning groups can operate smoothly, and thereby enhance learning. Students who cannot interact constructively with other students will not be able to take advantage of the learning opportunities provided by the cooperative learning situations and will furthermore deprive their fellow students of the opportunity for cooperative learning.

These skills form the hierarchy of cooperation in which students first learn to work together as a group, so they may then proceed to levels at which they may engage in simulated conflict situations. This cooperative setting allows different points of view to be constructively entertained.

Skill 6.3 The teacher applies a variety of instructional approaches to promote the development of higher-order thinking skills and encourage independent learning.

Higher-Ordered Thinking Skills

A critical thinking skill is a skill target that teachers help students develop to sustain learning in specific subject areas that can be applied within other subject areas. For example, when learning to understand algebraic concepts in solving a math word problem on how much fencing material is needed to build a fence around a backyard area that has a 8' x 12," a math student must understand the order of numerical expression in how to simplify algebraic expressions. Teachers can provide instructional strategies that show students how to group the fencing measurements into an algebraic word problem that with minor addition, subtraction and multiplication can produce a simple number equal to the amount of fencing materials needed to build the fence.

Developing critical thinking skills in students is not as simple as developing other simpler skills. In fact, many teachers mistakenly believe that these skills can be taught out of context (i.e., they can be taught as skills in and of themselves). Good teachers, however, realize that critical thinking skills must be taught within the contexts of specific subject matter. For example, Language Arts teachers can teach critical thinking skills through novels; Social Studies teachers can teach critical thinking skills through primary source documents or current events; Science teachers can teach critical thinking skills by having students develop hypotheses prior to conducting experiments.

First, let's start with definitions of the various types of critical thinking skills. Analysis is the systematic exploration of a concept, event, term, piece of writing, element of media, or any other complex item. Usually, people think of analysis as the exploration of the parts that make up a whole. For example, when someone analyzes a piece of literature, that person might focus on small pieces of the literature; yet, as they focus on the small pieces, they also call attention to the big picture and show how the small pieces create significance for the whole novel.

To carry this example further, if one were to analyze a novel, that person might investigate a particular character to determine how that character adds significance to the whole novel. In something more concrete like biology, one could analyze the findings of an experiment to see if the results might indicate significance for something even larger than the experiment itself. It is very easy to analyze political events, for example. A social studies teacher could ask students to analyze the events leading up to World War II: doing so would require that students look at the small pieces (e.g., smaller world events prior to World War II) and determine how those small pieces, when added up together, caused the war.

TEACHER STUDY GUIDE

Next, let's consider synthesis. Synthesis is usually thought of to be the opposite of analysis. In analysis, we take a whole and break it up into pieces and look at the pieces. With synthesis, we take different things and make them one whole thing. For example, a Language Arts teacher could ask students to synthesize two works of distinct literature. Let's say that we take *The Scarlett Letter* and *The Crucible*, two works both featuring life during Puritanical America, written about one century apart. A student could synthesize the two works and come to conclusions about Puritanical life. An Art teacher could ask students to synthesize two paintings from the Impressionist era and come to conclusions about the features that distinguish that style of art.

Finally, evaluation involves making judgments. Whereas analysis and synthesis seek answers and hypotheses based on investigations, evaluation seeks opinions. For example, a social studies teacher could ask students to evaluate the quality of Richard Nixon's resignation speech. To do so, they would judge whether or not they felt it was good. In contrast, analysis would keep judgment out of the assignment: it would have students focus possibly on the structure of the speech (i.e., Does an argument move from emotional to logical?). When evaluating a speech, a piece of literature, a movie, or a work of art, we seek to determine whether one thinks it is good or not. But, keep in mind, teaching good evaluation skills requires not just that students learn how to determine whether something is good or not—it requires that they learn how to support their evaluations. So, if a student claims that Nixon's speech was effective in what the President intended the speech to do, the student would need to explain how this is so. Notice that evaluation will probably utilize the skills of analysis and/or synthesis, but that the purpose is ultimately different.

In general, critical thinking skills should be taught through assignments, activities, lessons, and discussions that cause students to think on their own. While teachers can and should provide students with the tools to think critically, they will ultimately become critical thinkers if they have to use those tools themselves. But, this one last point cannot be taken lightly: Teachers must provide students the tools to evaluate, analyze, and synthesize.

Let's take political speeches as an example. Students will be better analyzers, synthesizers, and evaluators if they understand some of the basics of political speeches. Therefore, a teacher might introduce concepts such as rhetoric, style, persona, audience, diction, imagery, and tone. The best way to introduce these concepts would be to provide students with multiple, good examples of these things. Once they are familiar with these critical tools, students will be in a better place to apply them individually to political speeches—and then be able to analyze, synthesize, and evaluate political speeches on their own.

OPTE

TEACHER STUDY GUIDE

Encouraging Independent Critical Thinking

Since most teachers want their educational objectives to use higher level thinking skills, teachers need to direct students to these higher levels on the taxonomy. Questioning is an effective tool to build up students to these higher levels.

Low order questions are useful to begin the process. They insure the student is focused on the required information and understands what needs to be included in the thinking process. For example, if the objective is for students to be able to read and understand the story "Goldilocks and the Three Bears," the teacher may wish to start with low order questions (i.e., "What are some things Goldilocks did while in the bears home?" [Knowledge] or "Why didn't Goldilocks like the Papa Bear's chair?" [Analysis]).

Through a series of questions, the teacher can move the students up the taxonomy. (For example, "If Goldilocks had come to your house, what are some things she may have used?" [Application], "How might the story differed if Goldilocks had visited the three fishes?" [Synthesis], or "Do you think Goldilocks was good or bad? Why?" [Evaluation]). The teacher through questioning can control the thinking process of the class. As students become more involved in the discussion they are systematically being lead to higher level thinking.

To develop a critical-thinking approach to the world, children need to know enough about valid and invalid reasoning to ask questions. Bringing into the classroom speeches or essays that demonstrate both valid and invalid examples can be useful in helping students develop the ability to question the reasoning of others. These will be published writers or televised speakers, so they can see that they are able even to question ideas that are accepted by some adults and talk about what is wrong in the thinking of those apparently successful communicators.

If the teacher stays right on the cutting edge of children's experience, they will become more and more curious about what is out there in the world that they don't know about. A lesson on a particular country or even a tribe in the world that the children may not even know exists that will use various kinds of media to reveal to them what life is like there for children their own age is a good way to introduce the world out there. In such a presentation, positive aspects of the lives of those "other" children should be included. Perhaps a correspondence with a village could be developed. It's good for children, some of whom may not live very high on the social scale in this country, to know what the rest of the world is like, and in so doing, develop an independent curiosity to know more.

Skill 6.4 The teacher analyzes how various teacher roles (e.g., instructor, facilitator, coach, audience) and student roles (e.g., self-directed learner, group participant, passive observer) may affect learning processes and outcomes.

The Teacher's Role

Teaching consists of a multitude of roles. Teachers must plan and deliver instruction in a creative and innovating way so that students find learning both fun and intriguing. The teacher must also research various learning strategies, decide which to implement in the classroom, and balance that information according to the various learning styles of the students. Teachers must facilitate all aspects of the lesson including preparation and organization of materials, delivery of instruction, and management of student behavior and attention. Simultaneously, the teacher must also observe for student learning, interactions, and on-task behavior while making mental or written notes regarding what is working in the lesson and how the students are receiving and utilizing the information. This will provide the teacher with immediate feedback as to whether to continue with the lesson, or if it is necessary to slow the instruction or present the lesson in another way. Teachers must also work collaboratively with other adults in the room and utilize them to maximize student learning. The teacher's job requires the teacher to establish a delicate balance among all these factors.

How the teacher handles this balance depends on the teaching style of the teacher and/or lesson. Cooperative learning will require the teacher to have organized materials ready, perhaps even with instructions for the students as well. The teacher should conduct a great deal of observations during this type of lesson. Direct instruction methods will require the teacher to have an enthusiastic, yet organized, approach to the lesson. When teaching directly to students, the teacher must take care to keep the lesson student-centered and intriguing while presenting accurate information.

The Student's Role

Like the teacher, the student has more than role in a child-centered classroom. In collaborative settings, each student is expected to participate in class or group discussions. Through participation, students begin to realize their contributions have a place in a comprehensive discussion of a topic. Participation engages students in active learning, while increasing their self-confidence as they realize their ideas are necessary for group success.

Students also play the role of observer. As previously stated, behavioral theorists believe that through observation, a human's mind begins to make sense of the world around them as they decide to mimic or avoid certain behaviors. In a classroom, students observe many positive outcomes from behavior, as well as questioning, discussion and hands-on activities.

TEACHER STUDY GUIDE

An important goal for students should be to become self-directed in their learning. Teachers help students obtain this goal by providing them with ample opportunities to seek out their academic interests with various types of projects and assignments. Self-directed learners gain a lot from their inquiries since the topic usually interests them, and when student's take over certain aspects of their own education, they gain a sense of empowerment and ownership over their learning. This is an important role in the classroom because the sense of ownership promotes a sense of lifelong learning in students.

Skill 6.5 The teacher recognizes ways to enhance learning through the use of print, manipulative, technological, and human resources (e.g., primary documents, unit-counting blocks, computers and other educational technologies, community experts).

In considering suitable learning materials for the classroom, the teacher must have a thorough understanding of the state-mandated competency-based curriculum. According to state requirements, certain objectives must be met in each subject taught at every designated level of instruction. It is necessary that the teacher become well acquainted with the curriculum for which he/she is assigned. The teacher must also be aware that it is unlawful to require students to study from textbooks or materials other than those approved by the state Department of Education.

The bridge to effective learning for students begins with a collaborative approach by all stakeholders that support the educational needs of students. Underestimating the power and integral role of the community institutions in impacting the current and future goals of students can carry high stakes for students beyond the high school years who are competing for college access, student internships, and entry level jobs in the community. Researchers have shown that school involvement and connections with community institutions have greater retention rates of students graduating and seeking higher education experiences. The current disconnect and autonomy that has become commonplace in today's society must be reevaluated in terms of promoting tomorrow's citizens.

Unit Counting Blocks
Unit blocks as part of play or guided instruction provide children with the opportunity to relate to and manipulate objects with predictable similarities and relationships. Young children use the blocks to sort and order, and improve their motor skills. Older children can build increasingly complex structures modeled on what they've observed in their lives, as they continue to absorb more advanced concepts of geometry, such as shapes, symmetry and spatial relationships. As they progress, children begin building abstract designs and structures by manipulating patterns and experimenting with the inherent properties of the blocks.

TEACHER STUDY GUIDE

Over time, children can be guided from an inherent to an explicit understanding of these concepts, as knowledge is applied to the real world.

Community

When community institutions provide students and teachers with meaningful connections and input, the commitment is apparent in terms of volunteering, loyalty and professional promotion. Providing students with placements in leadership positions such as the ASB (Associated Student Body); the PTSA (Parent Teacher Student Association); School Boards; neighborhood sub-committees addressing political or social issues; or government boards that impact and influence school communities creates an avenue for students to explore ethical, participatory, collaborative, transformational leadership that can be applied to all areas of a student's educational and personal life.

Community liaisons provide students with opportunities to experience accountability and responsibility so that students learn about life and how organizations work with effective communication and teams working together to accomplish goals and objectives. Teaching students skills of inclusion, social and environmental responsibility and creating public forums that represent student voice and vote foster student interest and access to developing and reflecting on individual opinions and understanding the dynamics of the world around them.

When a student sees that the various support systems are in place and consistently working as a team to effectively provide resources and avenues of academic promotion and accountability, students have no fear of taking risks to grow by becoming a teen voice on a local committee about "Teen Violence" or volunteering in a local hospice for young children with terminal diseases. The linkages of community institutions provide role-models of a world in which the student will soon become an integral and vital member, so being a part of that world as a student makes the transition easier as a young adult.

Local experts

Most students accept what their own teacher tells them without questioning although not all do. The teacher's credibility expands when students have an opportunity to hear another "expert" talk about the same information. For example, if students are studying water animals, having the director of a fish hatchery visit the class and present his work will increase student interest and understanding. People are usually willing to give their time in this way, and there is reciprocal gain. The person speaking to the students gains satisfaction from passing on his/her own knowledge and expertise, and the students gain a new dimension on the topic they're discussing.

OPTE

Primary documents

Another way to increase student interest is in the use of primary documents. In a local history lesson, bringing in old documents from the court house or the library will increase students' interest in their own community and its history and possibly geography, especially if there are old, original maps. While it's not possible to bring the Declaration of Independence into the classroom, photo facsimiles are available and can have the same result as an original document. If students have taken trips to famous places and can report on seeing original documents, this also increases interest.

Field trips

Parents sometimes see field trips as a ploy on the part of a teacher to avoid the responsibility of managing children in the classroom. Nothing could be farther from the truth. Some of the richest learning can take place when students have an opportunity to get out of the classroom and participate in an eyes-on, even hands-on experience related to the topic they are studying at the time.

Service learning

Service learning has all the advantages of a field trip plus the opportunity for the students whose parents seldom make demands on them to meet another person's needs to experience altruism for themselves for the first time. Sometimes children are so impacted by this opportunity that they eventually choose careers of service to others. There have been many instances when children have visited a nursing home and find such fulfillment in the joy they were able to bring into the lives of unfortunate people that they ultimately choose the field of geriatrics for their life's work.

Keeping in mind the state requirements concerning the objectives and materials, the teacher must determine the abilities of the incoming students assigned to his/her class or supervision. It is essential to be aware of their entry behavior—that is, their current level of achievement in the relevant areas. The next step is to take a broad overview of students who are expected to learn before they are passed on to the next grade or level of instruction. Finally, the teacher must design a course of study that will enable students to reach the necessary level of achievement, as displayed in their final assessments, or exit behaviors. Textbooks and learning materials must be chosen to fit into this context.

To determine the abilities of incoming students, it may be helpful to consult their prior academic records. Letter grades assigned at previous levels of instruction as well as scores on standardized tests may be taken into account. In addition, the teacher may choose to administer pre-tests at the beginning of the school year, and perhaps also at the initial stage of each new unit of instruction. The textbooks available for classroom use may provide suitable pre-tests, tests of student progress, and post-tests.

TEACHER STUDY GUIDE

In selecting tests and other assessment tools, the teacher should keep in mind that different kinds of tests measure different aspects of student development. The tests included in most textbooks chosen for the classroom, and in the teacher's book that accompanies them are usually achievement tests. Few of these are the type of tests intended to measure the students' inherent ability or aptitude. Teachers will find it difficult to raise students' scores on ability tests, but students' scores on achievement tests may be expected to improve with proper instruction and application in the area being studied.

In addition to administering tests, the teacher may assess the readiness of students for a particular level of instruction by having them demonstrate their ability to perform some relevant task. In a class that emphasizes written composition, for example, students may be asked to submit writing samples. These may be used not only to assure the placement of the students into the proper level, but as a diagnostic tool to help them understand what aspects of their composition skills may need improvement. In the like manner, students in a speech class may be asked to make an impromptu oral presentation before beginning a new level or specific level of instruction. Others may be asked to demonstrate their psychomotor skills in a physical education class, display their computational skills in a mathematics class, and so on. Whatever the chosen task, the teacher will need to select or devise an appropriate assessment scale and interpret the results with care.

If students are informed their entry behaviors on such a scale, they will be better motivated, especially if they are able to observe their progress by some objective means at suitable intervals during the course. For this reason, it may be advisable to record the results of such assessments in the student's portfolios as well as in the teacher's records.

Teachers may also gauge student readiness by simply asking them about their previous experience or knowledge of the subject or task at hand. While their comments may not be completely reliable indicators of what they know or understand, such discussions have the advantage of providing an idea of the students' interest in what is being taught. Teachers can have little impact unless they are able to demonstrate how the material being introduced is relevant to the students' lives.

Textbooks
Most teachers chose to use textbooks, which are suitable to the age and developmental level of specific student populations. Textbooks reflect the values and assumptions of the society that produces them, while they also represent the knowledge and skills considered to be essential in becoming an educated adult. Finally, textbooks are useful to the school bureaucracy and the community, for they make public and accessible the private world of the classroom.

OPTE

Though these factors may favor the adoption of textbooks, the individual teacher may have only limited choice about which textbooks to use, since such decisions are often made by the school administration or the local school district (in observance of the state guidelines). If teachers are consulted about textbook selection, it is likely that they have little training in evaluation techniques, and they are seldom granted leave time to encourage informed decisions. On those occasions when teachers are asked to assist in the selection process, they should ask, above all, whether the textbooks have real substance—is World War II accurately chronicled, does the science textbook correctly conceptualize electrical current, do literary selections reflect a full range of genre?

Technological Resources

Microcomputers are now commonplace, and some schools can now afford laser discs to bring alive the content of a reference book in text, motion, and sound. Hand-held calculators eliminate the need for drill and practice in number facts, while they also support a problem solving and process to mathematics. Videocassettes (VCR's) are common and permit the use of home-produced or commercially produced tapes. Textbook publishers often provide films, recordings, and software to accompany the text, as well as maps, graphics, and colorful posters to help students visualize what is being taught. Teachers can usually scan the educational publishers' brochures that arrive at their principal's or department head's office on a frequent basis. Another way to stay current in the field is by attending workshops or conferences. Teachers will be enthusiastically welcomed on those occasions when educational publishers are asked to display their latest productions and revised editions of materials.

In addition, yesterday's libraries are today's media centers. Teachers can usually have opaque projectors delivered to the classroom to project print or pictorial images (including student work) onto a screen for classroom viewing. Some teachers have chosen to replace chalkboards with projectors that reproduce the print or images present on the plastic sheets known as transparencies, which the teacher can write on during a presentation or have machine-printed in advance. In either case, the transparency can easily be stored for later use. In an art or photography class, or any class in which it is helpful to display visual materials, slides can easily be projected onto a wall or a screen. Cameras are inexpensive enough to enable students to photograph and display their own work, as well as keep a record of their achievements in teacher files or student portfolios.

TEACHER STUDY GUIDE

Studies have shown that students learn best when what is taught in lecture and textbook reading is presented more than once in various formats. In some instances, students themselves may be asked to reinforce what they have learned by completing some original production—for example, by drawing pictures to explain some scientific process, by writing a monologue or dialogue to express what some historical figure might have said on some occasion, by devising a board game to challenge the players' mathematical skills, or by acting out (and perhaps filming) episodes from a classroom reading selection. Students usually enjoy having their work displayed or presented to an audience of peers. Thus, their productions may supplement and personalize the learning experiences that the teacher has planned for them.

Competency 0007
The teacher develops knowledge of and uses a variety of effective communication techniques to foster active inquiry, collaboration, and supportive interaction in the classroom.

Skill 7.1 The teacher applies strategies for adapting communication to facilitate student understanding (e.g., providing examples; simplifying complex problems; using visual, aural, and kinesthetic cues).

Generally speaking, concepts can be taught in two manners: deductively or inductively. In a deductive manner, the teacher gives a definition along with one or two examples and one or two non-examples. As a means of checking understanding, the teacher will ask the students to give additional examples or non-examples and perhaps to repeat the definition. In an inductive manner, the students will derive the definition from examples and non-examples provided by the teacher. The students will test these examples and non-examples to ascertain if they possess the attributes that meet the criteria of the definition.

It cannot be assumed that students are gaining meaning through definitions. It is quite possible that some students are able to memorize definitions without actually understanding the concept. If students understand concepts and gain meaning from definitions, they will be able to apply this information by giving both examples and non-examples. Students will further be able to list attributes and recognize related concepts. Research indicates that when students gain knowledge through instruction that includes a combination of giving definitions, examples, non-examples, and by identifying attributes, they are more likely to grasp complicated concepts than by other instructional methods.

Several studies have been carried out to determine the effectiveness of giving examples as well as the difference in effectiveness of various types of examples. It was found conclusively that the most effective method of concept presentation included giving a definition along with examples and non-examples and also providing an explanation of the examples and non-examples. These same studies indicate that boring examples were just as effective as interesting examples in promoting learning.

Additional studies have been conducted to determine the most effective number of examples that will result in maximum student learning. These studies concluded that a few thoughtfully selected examples are just as effective as several examples. It was determined that the actual number of examples necessary to promote student learning was relative to the learning characteristics of the learners. It was again ascertained that learning is facilitated when examples are provided along with the definition.

TEACHER STUDY GUIDE

Learning is further enhanced when critical attributes are listed along with a definition, examples, and non-examples. Classifying attributes is an effective strategy for both very young students and older students. According to Piaget's pre-operational phase of development, children learn concepts informally through experiences with objects just as they naturally acquire language. One of the most effective learning experiences with objects is learning to classify objects by a single obvious feature or attribute. Children classify objects typically, often without any prompting or directions. This natural inclination to classify objects carries over to classifying attributes of a particular concept and contributes to the student's understanding of concepts.

In order to facilitate understanding, the teacher uses visual cues to teach. These include providing a large amount of visual directions, giving demonstrations; utilizing matching games, charts, and graphs; utilizing maps and giving instruction on how to use a legend; utilizing color coded systems; utilizing number frames and abacuses; having the student look for words, letters, and pictures in papers and magazines; utilizing clues such as a green circle to begin and a red circle to stop; and having the student utilize rulers and number lines to develop understanding of numeracy concepts.

The teacher also uses kinesthetic cues to teach students. Kinesthetic learners need to move their bodies to learn best, stimulating their large or small muscles as they learn. They are hands-on learners who learn by doing and concentrate better when movement is involved. Teachers can incorporate strategies for kinesthetic learners by using movement exploration when teaching concepts, such as allowing students to climb on the monkey bars while learning to add or subtract; have students clap or tap out numbers and syllables; use human number lines or floor number lines so student can use heavy objects next to the line for physical feedback. Students should use a lot of manipulatives whenever possible and perform a lot of tasks with their eyes shut utilizing three-dimensional letters. They should use concrete objects for counting, sequencing, and establishing patterns.

The teacher should also use aural cues for the aural learners in the class. Students should be taught how to talk through tasks, they should be allowed to spell out loud and hear themselves say syllables out loud. The student should be required to state punctuation marks while reading to develop their awareness of how the mark is used. They should play a large variety of rhyming games and be encouraged to think out loud. They should also tape record lessons and tests.

TEACHER STUDY GUIDE

Skill 7.2 The teacher fosters students' expressive and receptive communication skills by modeling effective strategies for conveying information, collaborating, questioning, and responding.

Various studies have shown that learning is increased when the teacher acknowledges and amplifies the student responses. Additionally, this can be even more effective if the teacher takes one student's response and directs it to another student for further comment. When this occurs, the students acquire greater subject matter knowledge. This is due to a number of factors. One is that the student feels that he or she is a valuable contributor to the lesson. Another is that all students are forced to pay attention because they never know when they will be called on: group-alert. The teacher achieves group alert by stating the question, allowing for a pause time for the students to process the question and formulate an answer, and then calling on someone to answer. If the teacher calls on someone before stating the question, the rest of the students tune-out because they know they are not responsible for the answer. Teachers are advised to also alert the non-performers to pay attention because they may be called on to elaborate on the answer. Non-performers are defined as all the students not chosen to answer.

The idea of directing the student comment to another student is a valuable tool for engaging the lower achieving student. If the teacher can illicit even part of an answer from a lower-achieving student and then move the spotlight off of that student onto another student, the lower achieving student will be more likely to engage in the class discussion the next time. This is because they were not put "on the spot" for very long and they successfully contributed to the class discussion.

Additionally, the teacher shows acceptance and gives value to student responses by acknowledging, amplifying, discussing or restating the comment or question. If you allow a student response, even if it is blurted out, you must acknowledge the student response and tell the student the quality of the response. For example: The teacher asks, "Is chalk a noun?" During the pause time a student says, "Oh, so my bike is a noun." Without breaking the concentration of the class, the teacher looks to the student, nods and then places his or her index finger to the lips as a signal for the student not to speak out of turn and then calls on someone to respond to the original question. If the blurted out response is incorrect or needs further elaboration, the teacher may just hold up his or her index finger as an indication to the student that the class will address that in a minute when the class is finished with the current question.

A teacher acknowledges a student response by commenting on it. For example, the teacher states the definition of a noun, and then asks for examples of nouns in the classroom. A student responds, "My pencil is a noun." The teacher answers, "Okay, let us list that on the board." By this response and the action of writing "pencil" on the board, the teacher has just incorporated the student's response into the lesson.

A teacher may also amplify the student response through another question directed to either the original student or to another student. For example, the teacher may say, "Okay", giving the student feedback on the quality of the answer, and then add, "What do you mean by "run" when you say the battery runs the radio?"

Another way of showing acceptance and value of student response is to discuss the student response. For example, after a student responds, the teacher would say, "Class, let us think along that line. What is some evidence that proves what Susie just stated?"

And finally, the teacher may restate the response. For example, the teacher might say, "So you are saying, the seasons are caused by the tilt of the earth. Is this what you said?"

Therefore, a teacher keeps students involved by utilization of group-alert. Additionally, the teacher shows acceptance and value of student responses by acknowledging, amplifying, discussing or restating the response. This contributes to maintaining academic focus.

Beginning-teacher training explains that the focus of the classroom discussion should be on the subject matter and controlled by teacher-posed questions. When a student response is correct, it is not difficult to maintain academic focus. However, when the student response is incorrect, this task is a little more difficult. The teacher must redirect the discussion to the task at hand, and at the same time not devalue the student response. It is risky to respond in a classroom.

If a student is ridiculed or embarrassed by an incorrect response, the student my shut down and not participate thereafter in classroom discussion. One way to respond to the incorrect answer is to ask the child, "Show me from your book why you think that." This gives the student a chance to correct the answer and redeem himself or herself. Another possible response from the teacher is to use the answer as a non-example. For example, after discussing the characteristics of warm-blooded and cold-blooded animals, the teacher asks for some examples of warm-blooded animals. A student raises his or her hand and responds, "A snake." The teacher could then say, "Remember, snakes lay eggs; they do not have live birth. However, a snake is a good non-example of a mammal." The teacher then draws a line down the board and under a heading of "non-example" writes "snake." This action conveys to the child that even though the answer was wrong, it still contributed positively to the class discussion. Notice how the teacher did not digress from the task of listing warm-blooded animals, which in other words is maintaining academic focus, and at the same time allowed the student to maintain dignity.

It is more difficult for the teacher to avoid digression when a student poses a non-academic question. For example, during the classroom discussion of Romeo and Juliet, the teacher asks "Who told Romeo Juliet's identity?" A student raises his or her hand and asks, "May I go to the rest room?" The teacher could respond in one of two ways. If the teacher did not feel this was a genuine need, he or she could simply shake his or her head no while repeating the question, "Who told Romeo Juliet's identity?" If the teacher felt this was a genuine need and could not have waited until a more appropriate time, he or she may hold up the index finger indicating "just a minute," and illicit a response to the academic question from another student. Then, during the next academic question's pause-time, the teacher could hand the student the bathroom pass.

Skill 7.3 The teacher interacts with students in ways that demonstrate respect for and sensitivity to individual differences.

In personalized learning communities, relationships and connections between students, staff, parents and community members promote lifelong learning for all students. School communities that promote an inclusion of diversity in the classroom, community, curriculum and connections enable students to maximize their academic capabilities and educational opportunities. Setting school climates that are inclusive of the multicultural demographic student population create positive and proactive mission and vision themes that align student and staff expectations.

The following factors enable students and staff to emphasize and integrate diversity in student learning:
- Inclusion of multicultural themes in curriculum and assessments
- Creation of a learning environment that promotes multicultural research, learning, collaboration, and social construction of knowledge and application
- Providing learning tasks that emphasize student cognitive, critical thinking and problem-solving skills
- Learning tasks that personalize the cultural aspects of diversity and celebrate diversity in the subject matter and student projects
- Promotion of intercultural positive social peer interrelationships and connections

Teachers communicate diversity in instructional practices and experiential learning activities that create curiosity in students who want to understand the interrelationship of cultural experiences. Students become self-directed in discovering the global world in and outside the classroom. Teachers understand that when diversity becomes an integral part of the classroom environment, students become global thinkers and doers.

In the intercultural communication model, students are able to learn how different cultures engage in both verbal and nonverbal modes of communicating meaning. Students who become multilingual in understanding the stereotypes that have defined other cultures are able to create new bonding experiences that will typify a more integrated global culture. Students who understand how to effectively communicate with diverse cultural groups are able to maximize their own learning experiences by being able to transmit both verbally and non-verbally cues and expectations in project collaborations and in performance based activities.

The learning curve for teachers in intercultural understanding is exponential in that they are able to engage all learners in the academic process and learning engagement. Teaching students how to incorporate learning techniques from a cultural aspect enriches the cognitive expansion experience since students are able to expand their cultural knowledge bases.

Teachers must demonstrate respect for cultural diversity and individual differences by planning learning activities that are sensitive to issues of class, gender, race, ethnicity, family composition, age, and special needs. Teachers should look at the special characteristics of students within cultural contexts, using developmental and pedagogical knowledge to continuously refine teaching practices.

The teacher should treat students fairly, acknowledging the individual differences that make one student different from another and taking these differences into account. Teachers should modify their instruction based on observation and knowledge of their students' interests, abilities, skills, knowledge, family circumstances, and peer relationships. Teachers must take into account the impact of context and culture on behavior. They should enhance student's self esteem, motivation, character, and their respect for individual, cultural, religious and racial differences.

Teacher's should appreciate individual variation within each area of development, show respect for the diverse talents of all learners, and remain committed to helping them develop self-confidence and competence.

Teacher's should appreciate the cultural dimensions of communication, and respond appropriately, and attempt to develop culturally sensitive communication between students.

TEACHER STUDY GUIDE

Skill 7.4 The teacher understands how to use a variety of communication tools, including computers and other educational technologies, to enrich learning

Resources and materials for instruction are everywhere—in schools, on the web, in bookstores, and in adopted school programs. How does one decide where to get materials for instruction? And how does one evaluate materials for use in instruction?

The Internet and other research resources provide a wealth of information on thousands of interesting topics for students preparing presentations or projects. Using search engines like Google, Microsoft and Infotrac, student can search multiple Internet resources on one subject search. Students should have an outline of the purpose of a project or research presentation that includes:

- Purpose - identity the reason for the research information
- Objective - having a clear thesis for a project will allow the students opportunities to be specific on Internet searches
- Preparation - when using resources or collecting data, students should create folders for sorting through the information. Providing labels for the folders will create a system of organization that will make construction of the final project or presentation easier and less time consuming
- Procedure - organized folders and a procedural list of what the project or presentation needs to include will create A+ work for students and A+ grading for teachers
- Visuals or artifacts - choose data or visuals that are specific to the subject content or presentation. Make sure that poster boards or Power Point presentations can be visually seen from all areas of the classroom. Teachers can provide laptop computers for Power Point presentations.

When a teacher models and instructs students in the proper use of search techniques, the teacher can minimize wasted time in preparing projects and wasted paper from students who print every search. In some school districts, students are allowed a minimum number of printed pages per week. Since students have Internet accounts for computer usage, the monitoring of printing is easily done by the school's librarian and teachers in classrooms.

Having the school's librarian or technology expert be a guest speaker in classrooms provides another method of sharing and modeling proper presentation preparation using technology. Teachers can also appoint technology experts from the students in a classroom to work with students on projects and presentations. In high schools, technology classes provide students with upper-class teacher assistants who fill the role of technology assistants.

OPTE

TEACHER STUDY GUIDE

The wealth of resources for teachers and students seeking to incorporate technology and structured planning for student presentations and projects is as diverse as the presentations. There is an expert in every classroom who is always willing to offer advice and instruction. In school communities, that expert starts with the teacher.

Many school districts have shared drives that contain multiple files of lesson and unit plans, curriculum maps, pacing guides, and assessment ideas. While these can be very beneficial, it is always a good idea to determine the intended use for such files and documents.

The best place to start is identifying the required materials that should be used in instruction. After that, many websites contain lesson plans and instructional ideas. Be careful, though, as some websites do not monitor the information places on their servers. While a lesson may have a creative title and purpose, it may not always serve the best purpose for your instructional agenda. In fact, there is no guarantee that such lessons are any good! Consider how you would adapt it, if your students would get something out of it, and if it seems inappropriate for your particular group of students.

When looking through shared drives, remote devices, and other online databases, it is important to understand who has posted information and what the information really is for. Often times, it might be for specialized programs within the district. It's always safest to ask!

Competency 0008
The teacher understands and uses a variety of assessment strategies to evaluate and modify the teaching/learning process ensuring the continuous intellectual, social, and physical development of the learner.

Skill 8.1 The teacher uses assessment to adapt teaching to address the intellectual, social, and physical development of the student.

Assessment is key to providing differentiated and appropriate instruction to all students. Teachers should use a variety of the following assessment techniques to determine the existing knowledge and skills, as well as the needs, of each student. Depending on the age of the student and the subject matter under consideration, diagnosis of readiness may be accomplished through pre-test, checklists, teacher observation, or student self-report. Diagnosis serves two related purposes—to identify those students who are not ready for the new instruction, and to identify for each student what prerequisite knowledge is lacking.

Student assessment is an integral part of the teaching-learning process. Identifying student, teacher, or program weaknesses is only significant if the information so obtained is used to remedy those concerns. Lesson materials and lesson delivery must be evaluated to determine relevant prerequisite skills and abilities. The teacher must be capable of determining whether a student's difficulties lie with the new information or with a lack of significant prior knowledge. The ultimate goal of any diagnostic or assessment endeavor is improved learning. Thus, instruction is adapted to the needs of the learner based on assessment information.

There are many ways to evaluate a child's knowledge and assess his/her learning needs. In recent years, the emphasis has shifted from "mastery testing" of isolated skills to authentic assessments of what children know. Authentic assessments allow the teacher to know more precisely what each individual student knows, can do, and needs to do. Authentic assessments can work for both the student and the teacher in becoming more responsible for learning.

One of the simplest most efficient ways for the teacher to get to know his/her students is to conduct an entry survey. This is a record that provides useful background information about the students as they enter a class or school. Collecting information through an entry survey will give valuable insights into a student's background knowledge and experience. Teachers can customize entry surveys according to the type of information considered valuable. Some of the information that may be incorporated include student's name and age, family members, health factors, special interests, strengths, needs, fears, etc., parent expectations, languages spoken in the home, what the child likes about school, etc.

At the beginning of each school term the teacher will likely feel compelled to conduct some informal evaluations in order to obtain a general awareness of his/her students. These informal evaluations should be the result of a learning activity rather than a "test" and may include classroom observations, collections of reading and writing samples, and notations about the students' cognitive abilities as demonstrated by classroom discussions and participation including the students' command of language. The value of these informal evaluations cannot be underestimated. These evaluations, if utilized effectively, will drive instruction and facilitate learning.

After initial informal evaluations have been conducted and appropriate instruction follows, teachers will need to fine tune individual evaluations in order to provide optimum learning experiences. Some of the same types of evaluations can be used on an ongoing basis to determine individual learning needs as were used to determine initial general learning needs. It is somewhat more difficult to choose an appropriate evaluation instrument for elementary-aged students than for older students. Therefore, teachers must be mindful of developmentally appropriate instruments. At the same time, teachers must be cognizant of the information that they wish to attain from a specific evaluation instrument. Ultimately, these two factors—students' developmental stage and the information to be derived—will determine which type of evaluation will be most appropriate and valuable. There are few commercially designed assessment tools that will prove to be as effective as the tool that is constructed by the teacher.

A simple-to-administer, information-rich evaluation of a child's reading strengths and weaknesses is the running reading record. "This technique for recording reading behavior is the most insightful, informative, and instructionally useful assessment procedure you can use for monitoring a child's progress in learning to read;" (Traill, 1993) The teacher uses a simple coding system to record what a child does while reading text out loud. At a later time the teacher can go back to the record and assess what the child knows about reading and what the teacher needs to address in an effort to help the student become a better reader.

If the teacher is evaluating a child's writing, it is a good idea to discourage the child from erasing his/her errors and to train the child to cross out errors with a single line so that the teacher can actually see the process that the student went through to complete a writing assignment. This writing becomes an important means of getting to know about students' writing and is an effective, valuable writing evaluation.

TEACHER STUDY GUIDE

Mathematics skills can be evaluated informally by observing students as they work at their seats or perform at the board. Teachers can see if the students know basic computation skills, if they understand place value, or if they transpose numbers simply by watching them as they solve computation problems. Some teachers may prefer to administer some basic computation "tests" to determine a student's mathematics strengths and weaknesses. Although these "tests" are not as effective or thorough in assessing students, they are quick and easy to administer.

Skill 8.2 The teacher understands the characteristics and appropriate uses of formal and informal assessments (e.g., criterion and norm-referenced instruments, teacher-designed classroom tests, portfolios, peer assessment, student self-assessment, observation)

The process of collecting, quantifying and qualifying student performance data using multiple assessment information on student learning is called assessment. A comprehensive assessment system must include a diversity of assessment tools such as norm-referenced, criterion-referenced, performance-based, or any student generated alternative assessments that can measure learning outcomes and goals for student achievement and success in school communities. There are mainly four kinds of assessment:

1. Observation: noticing someone and judging their action.
2. Informal continuous assessment - less structured. Informal continuous assessment is informal because it is informal - not formal like a test or exam. It is continuous because it occurs periodically - on a daily or weekly basis.
3. Informal continuous assessment: more structured means setting up assessment situations periodically. An assessment situation is an activity you organize so that the learners could be assessed. It could be a quiz. It could also be a group activity, where the participants will be assessed.
4. Formal assessment is a structured infrequent measure of learner achievement. It involves the use of test and exam. Exams are used to measure the learner's progress.

The purpose of informal assessment is to help our learners learn better. This form of assessment helps the teacher to how well the learners are learning and progressing. Informal assessment can be applied to home work assignments, field journals, daily class work, which are good indicators of student progress and comprehension.

Formal assessment on the other hand is highly structured keeping the learner in mind. It must be done at regular intervals and if the progress is not satisfactory, parent involvement is absolutely essential. A test or exam is a good example of formal assessment. A science project is also a formal assessment.

Examples of Formal Assessments

Norm-referenced Assessments

Norm-referenced tests (NRT) are used to classify student learners for homogenous groupings based on ability levels or basic skills into a ranking category. In many school communities, NRTs are used to classify students into AP (Advanced Placement), honors, regular or remedial classes that can significantly impact student future educational opportunities or success. NRTs are also used by national testing companies such as Iowa Test of Basic Skills (Riverside), Florida Achievement Test (McGraw-Hill) and other major test publishers to test a national sample of students to norm against standard test-takers. Stiggins (1994) states "Norm-referenced tests (NRT) are designed to highlight achievement differences between and among students to produce a dependable rank order of students across a continuum of achievement from high achievers to low achievers."

Educators may select NRTs to focus on student learners with lower basic skills which could limit the development of curriculum content that needs to provide students with academic learning's that accelerate student skills from basic to higher skill application to address the state assessments and core subject expectations. NRT ranking ranges from 1-99 with 25% of students scoring in the lower ranking of 1-25 and 25% of students scoring in the higher ranking of 76-99. Florida uses a variety of NRTs for student assessments that range from Iowa Basic Skills Testing to California Battery Achievement testing to measure student learning in reading and math.

Criterion-referenced Assessments

Criterion-referenced assessments looks at specific student learning goals and performance compared to a norm group of student learners. According to Bond (1996) "Educators or policy makers may choose to use a Criterion-referenced test (CRT) when they wish to see how well students have learned the knowledge and skills which they are expected to have mastered." Many school districts and state legislation use CRTs to ascertain whether schools are meeting national and state learning standards. The latest national educational mandate of "No Child Left Behind" (NCLB) and Adequate Yearly Progress (AYP) use CRTs to measure student learning, school performance, and school improvement goals as structured accountability expectations in school communities. CRTs are generally used in learning environments to reflect the effectiveness of curriculum implementation and learning outcomes.

TEACHER STUDY GUIDE

Performance-based Assessments
Performance-based assessments are currently being used in a number of state testing programs to measure the learning outcomes of individual students in subject content areas. Washington State uses performance-based assessments for the WASL (Washington Assessment of Student Learning) in Reading, Writing, Math and Science to measure student-learning performance. Attaching a graduation requirement to passing the required state assessment for the class of 2008 has created a high-stakes testing and educational accountability for both students and teachers in meeting the expected skill based requirements for 10th grade students taking the test.

In today's classrooms, performance-based assessments in core subject areas must have established and specific performance criteria that start with pre-testing in a subject area and maintain daily or weekly testing to gauge student learning goals and objectives. To understand a student's learning is to understand how a student processes information. Effective performance assessments will show the gaps or holes in student learning which allows for an intense concentration on providing fillers to bridge non-sequential learning gaps. Typical performance assessments include oral and written student work in the form of research papers, oral presentations, class projects, journals, student portfolio collections of work, and community service projects.

Examples of Informal Assessments

Anecdotal records
These are notes recorded by the teacher concerning an area of interest or concern with a particular student. These records should focus on observable behaviors and should be descriptive in nature. They should not include assumptions or speculations regarding effective areas such as motivation or interest. These records are usually compiled over a period of several days to several weeks.

Rating scales & checklists
These assessments are generally self-appraisal instruments completed by the students or observations-based instruments completed by the teacher. The focus of these is frequently on behavior or effective areas such as interest and motivation.

Portfolio assessment
The use of student portfolios for some aspect of assessment has become quite common. The purpose, nature, and policies of portfolio assessment vary greatly from one setting to another. In general, though, a student's portfolio contains samples of work collected over an extended period of time. The nature of the subject, age of the student, and scope of the portfolio, all contribute to the specific mechanics of analyzing, synthesizing, and otherwise evaluating the portfolio contents.

OPTE

In most cases, the student and teacher make joint decisions as to which work samples go into the student's portfolios. A collection of work compiled over an extended time period allows teacher, student, and parents to view the student's progress from a unique perspective. Qualitative changes over time can be readily apparent from work samples. Such changes are difficult to establish with strictly quantitative records typical of the scores recorded in the teacher's grade book.

Questioning

One of the most frequently occurring forms of assessment in the classroom is oral questioning by the teacher. As the teacher questions the students, she collects a great deal of information about the degree of student learning and potential sources of confusing for the students. While questioning is often viewed as a component of instructional methodology, it is also a powerful assessment tool.

Skill 8.3 The teacher understands measurement principles and assessment concepts (e.g., validity, reliability, bias)

Validity and Reliability

A desirable assessment is both reliable and valid. Without adequate reliability and validity, an assessment provides unusable results. A reliable assessment provides accurate and consistent results; there is little error from one time to the next. A valid assessment is one which tests what it intends to test.

Reliability is directly related to correlation. A perfect positive correlation equals + 1.00 and a perfect negative correlation equals -1.00. The reliability of an assessment tool is generally expressed as a decimal to two places (eg. 0.85). This decimal number describes the correlation that would be expected between two scores if the same student took the test two times.

Actually, there are several ways to estimate the reliability of an instrument. The method which is conceptually the most clear is the test-retested method. When the same test is administered again to the same students, if the test is perfectly reliable, each student will receive the same score each time. Even as the scores of individual students vary some from one time to the next, it is desirable for the rank order of the students to remain unchanged. Other methods of estimating reliability operate off of the same conceptual framework. Split-half methods divide a single test into two parts and compare them. Equivalent forms methods use two versions of the same test and compare test. With some types of assessment, such as essays and observation reports, reliability concerns also deal with the procedures and criteria used for scoring. The inter-rater reliability ask the question: How much will the results vary depending on who is scoring or rating the assessment data?

TEACHER STUDY GUIDE

There are three commonly described types of validity: Content validity, criterion validity, and construct validity. Content validity describes the degree to which a test actually tests, say, arithmetic. Story problems on an arithmetic test will lower is validity as a measure of arithmetic since reading ability will also be reflected in the results. However, note that it remains a valid test of the ability to solve story problems. Criterion validity is so named because of the concern with the test's ability to predict performance on another measure or test. For example, a college admissions test is highly valid if it predicts very accurately those students who will attain high GPAs at that college. The criterion in this case is college GPA. Construct validity is concerned with describing the usefulness or reality of what is being tested. The recent interest in multiple intelligences, instead of a single IQ score, is an example of the older construct of intelligence being reexamined as potentially several distinct constructs.

A student's readiness for a specific subject is not an absolute concept, but is determined by the relationship between the subject matter or topic and the student's prior knowledge, interest, motivation, attitude, experience and other similar factors.

Thus, the student's readiness to learn about the water cycle depends on whether the student already knows related concepts such as evaporation, condensation, and filtration. Readiness, then, implies that there is not a "gap" between what the student knows and the prerequisite knowledge base for learning.

A pretest designed to assess significant and related prerequisite skill and abilities is the most common method of identifying the student's readiness. This assessment should focus, not on the content to be introduced, but on prior knowledge judged to be necessary for understanding the new content. A pretest, which focuses on the new content, may identify students who do not need the new instruction (who have already mastered the material), but it will not identify students with readiness gaps.

TEACHER STUDY GUIDE

The most common areas of readiness concerns fall in the basic academic skill areas. Mastery of the basic skill areas is a prerequisite for almost all subject area learning. Arithmetic skills and some higher level mathematics skills are generally necessary for science learning or for understanding history and related time concepts. Reading skills are necessary throughout the school years and beyond. A student with poor reading skills is at a disadvantage when asked to read a textbook chapter independently. Writing skills, especially handwriting, spelling, punctuation, and mechanics, are directly related to success in any writing-based activity. A weakness in any of these basic skill areas may at first glance appear to be a difficulty in understanding the subject area. A teacher who attempts to help the student master the subject matter through additional emphasis on the content will be misusing instructional time and frustrating the student. An awareness of readiness issues helps the teacher to focus on treating the underlying deficiency instead of focusing on the overt symptoms.

Once a readiness gap has been identified, then the teacher can provide activities designed to close the gap. Specific activities may be of almost any form. Since most learning builds upon previous learning, there are few activities or segments of learning that can be viewed solely as readiness or non-readiness activities. In a very direct very few types of learning can be identified as solely readiness activities without legitimacy in their own right.

While growth and maturation rates vary greatly from individual to individual, there are some generalizations that can be made concerning development characteristics of children. Most children appear to go through identifiable, sequential stages of growth and maturation, although not at the same rate. For the curriculum developers, it is often necessary to make some generalizations about the development level of the students of a particular age group or grade level. These generalizations, then, provide a framework for establishing the expectations of the children's performance. Textbooks, scope and sequence charts, school curriculum planners, and more, translate these generalizations into plans and expectations for the students. The curriculum plan that emerges identifies general goals and expectations for the average student.

One of the teacher's responsibilities in this situation is to realize the nature of the initial rough estimate of what is appropriate for a given group of students. The teacher should expect to modify and adjust the instructional program based on the needs and abilities of the students. A teacher may do this by grouping students for alternative instruction, adjusting or varying the materials (textbooks), varying the teaching methods, or varying the learning tasks.

Bias

Bias exists in assessment when, after getting the results, it is obvious that demographic variables account for score variation. In other words, test bias would exist if a test question assumes that the test taker understands some of the contextual information in the question. For example, let's say a test question is trying to assess a student's understanding of a science concept that has been taught in class. However, the teacher uses an example to set up the question that assumes all students have the same cultural background. This test question would be assumed to be biased.

There are a few ways to systematically notice potential bias. First, when test questions are developed, they should focus on assessing discrete skills or areas of knowledge that have been taught. With teacher-created test materials, teachers should not include elements on the test that might require students to access information that they may not have. While some students possibly could know that additional information, not all students will, and it will instead look like those other students did not know the material the teacher really intended for the student to know. So, test questions should be simply written, contain basic vocabulary, and not include elements that pertain to any one culture or religion.

On a wider level, teachers may notice that an entire demographic group has performed worse compared to other demographic groups on a particular question. This might be a clue to possible bias.

How can teachers eliminate bias on their own assessments that they create? They can work ensure that everything tested has been taught. This is an important task. Teachers should carefully examine their tests for material that students would have no way of knowing. Teachers should also be very sensitive to the things that they take for granted. Something as simple as forgetting that different religions celebrate different holidays can lead to bias.

Skill 8.4 The teacher effectively interprets and communicates assessment results to students, parents/guardians, and colleagues.

Communicating with Students

How can a teacher provide good feedback so that students will learn from their assessments? First, language should be helpful and constructive. Critical language does not necessarily help students learn. They may become defensive or hurt, and therefore, they may be more focused on the perceptions than the content. Language that is constructive and helpful will guide students to specific actions and recommendations that would help them improve in the future.

When teachers provide timely feedback, they increase the chance that students will reflect on their thought-processes as they originally produced the work. When feedback comes weeks after the production of an assignment, the student may not remember what it is that caused him or her to respond in a particular way.

Specific feedback is particularly important. Comments like, "This should be clearer" and "Your grammar needs to be worked on" provide information that students may already know. They may already know they have a problem with clarity. What they can benefit from is commentary that provides very specific actions students could take to make something more clear or to improve his or her grammar.

When teachers provide feedback on a set of assignments, for example, they enhance their students' learning by teaching students how to use the feedback. For example, returning a set of papers can actually do more than provide feedback to students on their initial performance. Teachers can ask students to do additional things to work with their original products, or they can even ask students to take small sections and re-write based on the feedback. While written feedback will enhance student learning, having students do something with the feedback encourages even deeper learning and reflection.

Experienced teachers may be reading this and thinking, "When will I ever get the time to provide so much feedback?" Although detailed and timely feedback is important—and necessary—teachers do not have to provide it all the time to increase student learning. They can also teach students how to use scoring guides and rubrics to evaluate their own work, particularly before they turn it in. One particularly effective way of doing this is by having students examine models and samples of proficient work. Over years, teachers should collect samples, remove names and other identifying factors, and show these to students so that they understand what is expected of them. Often, when teachers do this, they will be surprised to see how much students gain from this in terms of their ability to assess their own performance.

Finally, teachers can help students develop plans for revising and improving upon their work, even if it is not evaluated by the teacher in the preliminary stages. For example, teachers can have students keep track of words they commonly misspell, or they can have students make personal lists of areas they feel on which they need to focus.

Communicating with Parents/Guardians

The major questions for parents in understanding student performance criterion-referenced data assessment are, "Are students learning?" and "How well are students learning?" Providing parents with a collection of student learning assessment data related to student achievement and performance is a quantifiable response to the questions.

TEACHER STUDY GUIDE

The National Study of School Evaluation (NSSE) 1997 research on School Improvement: Focusing on Student performance adds the following additional questions for parent focus on student learning outcomes:

- What are the types of assessments of student learning that are used in the school?
- What do the results of the data assessments indicate about the current levels of student learning performance? About future predictions? What were the learning objectives and goals?
- What are the strengths and limitations in student learning and achievement?
- How prepared are students for further education or promotion to the next level of education?
- What are the trends seen in student learning in various subject areas or overall academic learning?

Providing parents with opportunities to attend in-service workshops on data discussions with teachers and administrators creates additional opportunity for parents to ask questions and become actively involved in monitoring their student's educational progress. With state assessments, parents should look for the words "passed" or "met/exceeded standards" in interpreting the numerical data on student reports. Parents who maintain an active involvement in their students' education will attend school opportunities to promote their understanding of academic and educational achievement for students.

Communicating with Colleagues

When students leave a teacher's classroom, an accurate and updated file of information should follow them. The student permanent record is a file of the student's cumulative educational history. It contains a profile of the student's academic background as well as the student's behavioral and medical background. Other pertinent individual information contained in the permanent record includes the student's attendance, grade averages, and schools attended. Personal information such as parents' names and addresses, immunization records, child's height and weight, and narrative information about the child's progress and physical and mental well being is an important aspect of the permanent record. All information contained within the permanent record is strictly confidential and is only to be discussed with the student's parents or other involved school personnel.

The purpose of the permanent record is to provide applicable information about the student so that the student's individual educational needs can be met. If any specialized testing has been administered, the results are noted in the permanent record. Any special requirements that the student may have are indicated in the permanent record. Highly personal information, including court orders regarding custody, is filed in the permanent record as is appropriate. The importance and value of the permanent record cannot be underestimated. It offers a comprehensive knowledge of the student.

TEACHER STUDY GUIDE

The current teacher is responsible for maintaining the student's permanent record. All substantive information in regard to testing, academic performance, the student's medical condition, and personal events are placed in the permanent record file. Updated information in regard to the student's grades, attendance, and behavior is added annually. These files are kept in a locked fireproof room or file cabinet and cannot be removed from this room unless the person removing them signs a form acknowledging full responsibility for the safe return of the complete file. Again, only the student's parents (or legal guardians), the teacher or other concerned school personnel may view the contents of the permanent record file.

The permanent record file follows the student as he/she moves through the school system with information being updated along the way. Anytime the student leaves a school, the permanent record is transferred with the student. The permanent record is regarded as legal documentation of a student's educational experience.

See also Skill 5.4

TEACHER STUDY GUIDE

Competency 0009
The teacher shall have an understanding of the importance of assisting students with career awareness and the application of career concepts to the academic curriculum.

Skill 9.1 The teacher applies strategies to increase students' awareness of connections between academic learning and the workplace (e.g., introducing young children to different types of jobs, integrating authentic learning/work experiences into the curriculum, expanding students' knowledge of career opportunities).

Educators have recognized the necessity to more closely integrate academic and vocational learning, as the transition from school to work has proven a rocky road for students of the 21st century. With heavy academic loads and pressures to perform well on mandated tests, students find it increasingly difficult to find relevance in and connect to instructional content and apply it to their lives and the world around them.

For some students, the pressures of preparing for college – succeeding academically, volunteering in community service, participating in extracurricular activities – overshadow the actual purpose of college: to train for a career. They may reach their senior year of high school academically ready but largely unaware of and unprepared for the breadth of career choices available to them.

It's never too early to begin incorporating information about the working world into instruction and curriculum. One or more of a child's parents or caregivers likely has a job outside of the home, so the working world is already a part of the child's life and she has a context with which to discuss it.

In general, the effective teacher takes every opportunity to make real-world associations with a subject or lesson. The teacher should also explicitly make connections between an academic skill and the working world, and not simply assume the students will be able to make the connection on their own.

Authentic learning/work experiences
Expose students to key facets of the working world. The foundations of the subjects that students study were created and developed by professionals doing their jobs. Take every opportunity to show an active relationship between the students' textbooks and the world around them.

- Invite business and community leaders to speak about their careers. Have students prepare questions ahead of time: What does it take to perform their jobs, in terms of education and experience? How did they get started on their career path? What advice can they share with someone considering such a career?

- Arrange a field trip to a local business where students can observe the environment and speak with employees about their typical days. Ask a representative to describe the various jobs available within the company.
- Incorporate news and published works from the working world that are related to a lesson. When reading a novel in language arts class, include an interview with author about the writing process. For a unit in microbiology, include news of the latest scientific findings.

Expanding students' knowledge of career opportunities
- Find magazine or Internet articles listing different types of job groupings (e.g., the top paying jobs, the "hottest" jobs, hot jobs of the future) and use them as discussion points – why are they top paying/hot jobs, what skills do those jobs require, where can one obtain those skills, etc.
- During a larger lesson unit, make time to include a discussion about what jobs exist related to the instructional content. In a government class, a lesson on the U.S. Constitution can incorporate a discussion of jobs that maintain, enforce and protect the Constitution, such as Congress, the Senate, justices and judges, law enforcement officers, lawyers and paralegals.

Skill 9.2 The teacher understands how to involve employers and members of the community in career awareness and preparation activities.

Connecting with community resources will provide viable avenues of support in helping students who need additional academic remediation access learning. There are a diversity of programs that are offered through the local Universities and community agencies that connect college students or working adults with subject areas and classrooms in need of additional student interns/adult volunteers to support the academic programs in school communities.

According to Walther-Thomas et al (2000), "Collaboration for Inclusive Education," ongoing professional development that provides teachers with opportunities to create effective instructional practice is vital and necessary, "A comprehensive approach to professional development is perhaps the most critical dimension of sustained support for successful program implementation." The inclusive approach incorporates learning programs that include all stakeholders in defining and developing high quality programs for students. Figure 1 on the next page shows how an integrated approach of stakeholders can provide the optimal learning opportunity for all students.

Figure 1-Integrated Approach to Learning

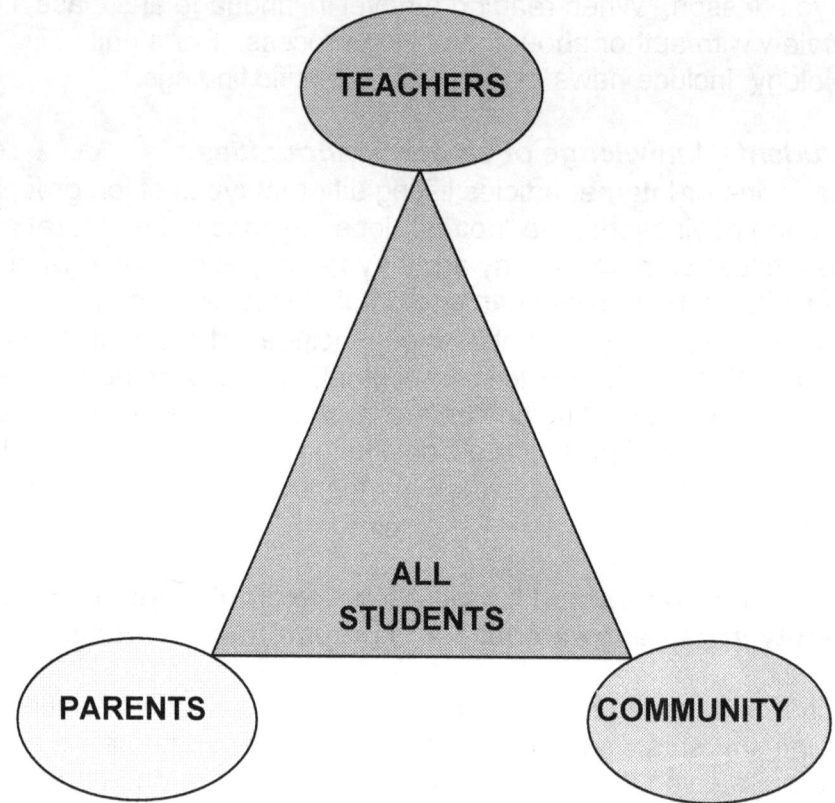

In the integrated approach to learning, teachers, parents, and community support become the integral apexes to student learning. The focus and central core of the school community is triangular as a representation of how effective collaboration can work in creating success for student learners. The goal of student learning and achievement now become the heart of the school community. The direction of teacher professional development in constructing effective instruction is clearly articulated in a greater understanding of facilitating learning strategies that develop skills and education equity for students.

TEACHER STUDY GUIDE

The bridge to effective learning for students begins with a collaborative approach by all stakeholders that support the educational needs of students. Underestimating the power and integral role of the community institutions in impacting the current and future goals of students can carry high stakes for students beyond the high school years who are competing for college access, student internships, and entry level jobs in the community. Researchers have shown that school involvement and connections with community institutions have greater retention rates of students graduating and seeking higher education experiences. The current disconnect and autonomy that has become commonplace in today's society must be reevaluated in terms of promoting tomorrow's citizens.

When community institutions provide students and teachers with meaningful connections and input, the commitment is apparent in terms of volunteering, loyalty and professional promotion. Providing students with placements in leadership positions such as the ASB (Associated Student Body); the PTSA (Parent Teacher Student Association); School Boards; neighborhood sub-committees addressing political or social issues; or government boards that impact and influence school communities creates an avenue for students to explore ethical, participatory, collaborative, transformational leadership that can be applied to all areas of a student's educational and personal life.

Community liaisons provide students with opportunities to experience accountability and responsibility so that students learn about life and how organizations work with effective communication and teams working together to accomplish goals and objectives. Teaching students skills of inclusion, social and environmental responsibility and creating public forums that represent student voice and vote foster student interest and access to developing and reflecting on individual opinions and understanding the dynamics of the world around them.

When a student sees that the various support systems are in place and consistently working as a team to effectively provide resources and avenues of academic promotion and accountability, students have no fear of taking risks to grow by becoming a teen voice on a local committee about "Teen Violence" or volunteering in a local hospice for young children with terminal diseases. The linkages of community institutions provide role-models of a world in which the student will soon become an integral and vital member, so being a part of that world as a student makes the transition easier as a young adult.

Research has shown that educators who collaborate become more diversified and effective in implementation of curriculum and assessment of effective instructional practices. The ability to gain additional insight into how students learn and modalities of differing learning styles can increase a teacher's capacity to develop proactive instruction methods. Teachers who team teacher or have daily networking opportunities can create a portfolio of curriculum articulation and inclusion for students.

People in business are always encouraged to network in order to further their careers. The same can be said for teaching. If English teachers get together and discuss what is going on in their classrooms, those discussions make the whole much stronger than the parts. Even if there are not formal opportunities for such networking, it's wise for schools or even individual teachers to develop them and seek them out.

Skill 9.3 The teacher plans and implements learning experiences to address racial, socio-economic, ethnic, and gender stereotyping related to careers.

A significant focus of career planning instruction should be to stimulate student awareness of the kinds of career options available to them and to offset any stereotypes (such as race, gender, or ethnicity stereotypes) that may limit their opinion about career prospects. Instructional resources should give students information about educational and other requirements connected to a range of occupations and career paths so that they have a clear understanding of what it will take to prepare for a specific career goal.

The resources used by the teacher should include descriptions of men and women in a wide range of occupations. The resources should take into account the avenues available and requirements of a variety of career opportunities. The resources used should also reflect people of different ethnicity and cultural backgrounds in atypical professions so that stereotypes are addressed and the range of career options is not linked to a specific group of people.

Professions should not be chosen or discussed based on the type of person who typically works in the profession. Students should be given a wide range of career opportunities and the career selections promoted should be linked to ability, interest, and demand for a particular career path.

Students should be given information on typical salaries, including starting salaries, educational requirements, and the job outlook.

Skill 9.4 The teacher plans and implements instructional activities that help students develop skills needed in the workplace (e.g., working in teams, problem solving, communication).

Students begin the directed development of thinking and participation skills right from the start, in kindergarten and elementary school. As they learn about and begin to engage in the world around them, many skills are needed to function effectively in the school setting, at home and within the community, such as sharing, cooperation, collaboration, problem-solving, and decision-making. The need for these skills never diminishes, and once a student enters the adult world, they're absolutely essential.

Similar to honing a talent at a particular task or hobby, these skills require practice. Also given that these skills are not necessarily easy or intuitive for the average person, it's unrealistic to expect that any student could absorb practice, and master these skills in high school or college alone and emerge from their educational experience ready to wield them successfully. Like any talent, the earlier these skills are introduced and the more they are practiced, the faster proficiency will develop.

SUBAREA III—THE PROFESSIONAL ENVIRONMENT

Competency 0010 The teacher evaluates the effects of his/her choices and actions on others (students, parents, and other professionals in the learning community), modifies those actions when needed, and actively seeks opportunities for continued professional growth.

Skill 10.1 The teacher applies strategies for self-assessment (e.g., with respect to effectiveness of instruction; relations with colleagues; gender, cultural, and other biases; and interactions with parents/guardians/family members).

Whether a teacher is using criterion-referenced, norm-referenced or performance-based data to inform and impact student learning and achievement, the more important objective is ensuring that teachers know how to effectively use the data to improve and reflect upon existing teaching instructions. The goal of identifying ways for teachers to use the school data is simple, "Is the teacher's instructional practice improving student learning goals and academic success?"

School data can include demographic profiling, cultural and ethic academic trends, state and/or national assessments, portfolios, academic subject pre-post assessment and weekly assessments, projects, and disciplinary reports. By looking at trends and discrepancies in school data, teachers can ascertain whether they are meeting the goals and objectives of the state, national, and federal mandates for school improvement reform and curriculum implementation.

Assessments can be used to motivate students to learn and shape the learning environment to provide learning stimulation that optimizes student access to learning. Butler and McMunn (2006) have shown that "factors that help motivate students to learn are 1) Involving students in their own assessment, 2) Matching assessment strategies to student learning, and 3) Consider thinking styles and using assessments to adjust the classroom environment in order to enhance student motivation to learn." Teachers can shape the way students learn by creating engaging learning opportunities that promote student achievement.

TEACHER STUDY GUIDE

Assessing one's own teaching strengths and weaknesses

The ultimate goal of teachers when they enter the profession of teaching is to provide a comprehensive education for all students by providing challenging curriculum and setting high expectations for learning. In an ideal classroom, the mechanisms for providing the perfect teaching climate and instruction are the norm and not the exception. Given the diversity of learners from a multitude of cultural, ethnic, intellectual, socioeconomic and grade level prepared backgrounds, the reality is that teachers are confronted with classrooms that are infused with classroom management issues and differentiated learning among learners who are either positively engaged in the learning process or negatively removed from all aspects of learning.

Researchers have shown that for new teachers entering the profession, the two greatest obstacles are dealing with increasing behavioral issues in the classroom and dealing with student minimally engaged in their own learning process. The goal of teachers is to maintain a toolkit of resources to deal with an ever-changing landscape of learners and classroom environments.

> (1) The educator's primary professional concern will always be for the student and for the development of the student's potential. The educator will therefore strive for professional growth and will seek to exercise the best professional judgment and integrity.

In a student-centered learning environment, the goal is to provide the best education and opportunity for academic success for all students. Integrating the developmental patterns of physical, social and academic norms for students will provide individual learners with student learning plans that are individualized and specific to their skill levels and needs. Teachers who effectively develop and maximize a student's potential will use pre- and post-assessments to gain comprehensive data on the existing skill level of the student in order to plan and adapt curriculum to address and grow student skills. Maintaining communication with the student and parents will provide a community approach to learning where all stakeholders are included to maximize student-learning growth.

> (2) Aware of the importance of maintaining the respect and confidence of one's colleagues, of students, of parents, and of other members of the community, the educator strives to achieve and sustain the highest degree of ethical conduct.

TEACHER STUDY GUIDE

The ethical conduct of an educator has undergone extensive scrutiny in today's classrooms. Teachers are under intense rules and regulations to maintain the highest degree of conduct and professionalism in the classroom. Current court cases have examined ethical violations of teachers engaged in improper communication and abuse with students, along with teachers engaged in drug violations and substance abuse in classrooms. It is imperative that teachers educating today's young people have the highest regard for professionalism and be proper role models for students in and out of the classrooms.

The very nature of the teaching profession—the yearly cycle of doing the same thing over and over again—creates the tendency to fossilize, to quit growing, to become complacent. The teachers who are truly successful are those who have built into their own approach to their jobs and to their lives safeguards against that. They see themselves as constant learners. They believe that learning never ends. They are careful never to teach their classes the same as they did the last time. They build in a tendency to reflect on what is happening to their students under their care or what happened this year as compared to last year. What worked the best? What didn't work so well? What can be changed to improve success rates? What about continuing education? Should they go for another degree or should they enroll in more classes?

There are several avenues a teacher might take in order to assess his or her own teaching strengths and weaknesses. Early indicators that a self-evaluation might be necessary include having several students that are not understanding a concept. In such a case, a teacher might want to go over his or her lesson plans to make sure the topic is being covered thoroughly and in a clear fashion. Brainstorming other ways to tackle the content might also help. Speaking to other teachers, asking how they teach a certain skill, might give new insight to one's own teaching tactics.

Any good teacher will understand that he or she needs to self-evaluate and adjust his or her lessons periodically. Signing up for professional courses or workshops can also help a teacher assess his or her abilities by opening one's eyes to new ways of teaching.

Family involvement is required for success in school. When parents volunteer their time and attention, students achieve more and enjoy school more. When conducting a self-assessment, the teacher should be evaluating whether or not they are doing all they can to create strong relationships with the parents of the students. Teachers should ask themselves if they actively encourage classroom visits and do they use parents as a resource to discover information about the students and also offer expertise in areas being taught.

OPTE

Other questions that should be asked include: Do you prepare for parent-teacher conferences ahead of time so that they are as comfortable and informative as possible? Do you maintain regular communication with parents outside of parent conferences and visitation days?

Another avenue that should be assessed by the teacher is the teacher's relationship with their colleagues. Teachers should assess their interactions with their colleagues to determine if they are working together appropriately, sharing resources, and doing things together to help for the betterment of the school. Additional aspects that should garner a self-analysis is whether the teacher communicates and interacts in a professional manner with the school community. Teachers should look at whether the documents they have written are done in a professional manner. They should also assess whether they have been providing clear oral and written instructions and whether they are utilizing their listening skills effectively. Teachers should also assess any biases that may be prevalent in their teaching to ensure that they are being fair to all students. An honest look into whether the teacher is able to demonstrate sensitivity to cultural, gender, intellectual, and physical ability differences in the classroom and in response to student's communications, is required.

Skill 10.2 The teacher understands how to evaluate and respond to feedback (e.g., from supervisors, students, parents/guardians, colleagues).

It has often been said that "everyone is a critic," and this is certainly true when one is a teacher. Students, other teachers, supervisors, parents—all will have something to say about the way you handle any given situation or subject. If you are hearing the same critiques from many different sources, then there is probably some truth behind what is being said. Take a step back and examine the criticism. Putting personal feelings aside is key; look at the mechanics of the problem. Work with your supervisor, your mentor, and/or your colleagues to restructure your lesson plans or your way of interacting with the students.

Even when a piece of feedback seems spurious, a fair response is to thank the person for their thoughts and say that you will take them into consideration. Always give the critic the benefit of the doubt; chances are they have your and your students' best interests at heart. If a discussion becomes heated, everyone will lose sight of the goal: to make your classes the best they can be so that your students meet the standards they need to meet in order to progress, learn, and grow.

The teacher is the manager of his classroom. This can seem a lonely business sometimes, especially when he has a particularly troubled or troubling student or group of students. Fortunately, he is not alone. He has colleagues who are usually more than willing to step in and help out. Sharing ownership of the classroom with other teachers who may be dealing with the same students makes this job tenable. If teachers are sharing the same student, they can, together, develop a strategy for dealing with that student. The same is true of parents. That relationship must not be adversarial unless there is no other way to handle the student and the situation.

In communications with other teachers, administration, and parents, respectful, reciprocal communication solves many problems. This is especially true if the teacher truly respects the opinions and ideas of others involved in the life of the students. The teacher may be the classroom expert, but parents may be the experts in what is going on with their child. Bringing them into the decision-making process in dealing with their child may lead to solutions and success beyond what the teacher could envision. The teacher may be the principal in the life of the child for a few hours each day five days a week nine months of the year, but the parents' role in the life of the child is constant. A sense of partnership between parents and teacher is vital and useful. When decisions are made regarding the management of the time of the child in the classroom, they should be shared decisions.

Skill 10.3 The teacher utilizes resources to promote professional growth (e.g., colleagues, professional associations, journals) and selects appropriate professional development activities (e.g., in-service training programs, continuing education)

Professional development opportunities for teacher performance improvement or enhancement in instructional practices are essential for creating comprehensive learning communities. In order to promote the vision, mission and action plans of school communities, teachers must be given the toolkits to maximize instructional performances. The development of student-centered learning communities that foster the academic capacities and learning synthesis for all students should be the fundamental goal of professional development for teachers.

TEACHER STUDY GUIDE

The level of professional development may include traditional district workshops that enhance instructional expectations for teachers or the more complicated multiple day workshops given by national and state educational organizations to enhance the federal accountability of skill and professional development for teachers. Most workshops on the national and state level provide clock hours that can be used to renew certifications for teachers every five years. Typically, 150 clock hours is the standard certification number needed to provide a five year certification renewal, so teachers must attend and complete paperwork for a diversity of workshops that range from 1-50 clock hours according to the timeframe of the workshops.

Most districts require that schools provide in-service professional development opportunities for teachers during the school year dealing with district objectives/expectations and relevant workshops or classes that can enhance the teaching practices for teachers. Clock hours are provided with each class or workshop and the type of professional development being offered to teachers determines clock hours. Each year, schools are required to report the number of workshops, along with the participants attending the workshops to the Superintendent's office for filing. Teachers collecting clock hour forms are required to file the forms to maintain certification eligibility and job eligibility.

The research by the National Association of Secondary Principals,' "Breaking Ranks II: Strategies for Leading High School Reform" created the following multiple listing of educational practices needed for expanding the professional development opportunities for teachers:

- Interdisciplinary instruction between subject areas
- Identification of individual learning styles to maximize student academic performance
- Training teachers in understanding and applying multiple assessment formats and implementations in curriculum and instruction
- Looking at multiple methods of classroom management strategies
- Providing teachers with national, federal, state and district curriculum expectations and performance outcomes
- Identifying the school communities' action plan of student learning objectives and teacher instructional practices
- Helping teachers understand how to use data to impact student learning goals and objectives
- Teaching teachers on how to disaggregate student data in improving instruction and curriculum implementation for student academic equity and access
- Develop leadership opportunities for teachers to become school and district trainers to promote effective learning communities for student achievement and success

OPTE

In promoting professional development opportunities for teachers that enhance student achievement, the bottom line is that teachers must be given the time to complete workshops at no or minimal costs. School and district budgets must include financial resources to support and encourage teachers to engage in mandatory and optional professional development opportunities that create a "win-win" learning experience for students.

Skill 10.4 The teacher collaborates with other members of the school community (e.g., other teachers, mentors, supervisors, special needs professionals, administrators, support staff) to enhance skills and solve problems.

Part of being an effective teacher is to not only get your students to grow educationally, but to allow oneself to also continue to grow. Working with other members of the school community—peers, supervisors, and other staff—will give you the grounding you need to increase your skills and knowledge sets. Identifying possible mentors, teachers you respect and whom you would like to emulate, is one step. Search out other teachers who have had an amount of success in the area you wish to learn more about. Ask them questions and for advice on brushing up your lesson plans. Talk to your supervisor or the principal when you are having difficulties, or when you want to learn more. They may know of development training seminars, books, journals, or other resources that might help you. Teachers should remember that they are part of a team of professionals, and that their personal success is part of a greater success that everyone hopes to achieve.

Mentors

Novice teachers can benefit greatly from access to effective mentors. Mentoring gives new teachers access to the expertise of their colleagues through their accumulated instructional and problem-solving knowledge and experience. A mentor's role is to guide the new teacher through the day-to-day reality of teaching in the classroom and to serve as a sounding board, a confidant, and a resource for good teaching practices. Further, an effective mentoring program boosts teacher retention rates, and both mentors and mentees often report increased job satisfaction.

See also Skill 9.2.

TEACHER STUDY GUIDE

Competency 0011 The teacher understands the State teacher evaluation process, "Oklahoma Criteria for Effective Teaching Performance," and how to incorporate these criteria in designing instructional strategies.

Skill 11.1 The teacher understands and incorporates state-mandated standards for teacher performance (e.g., instruction, scheduling, record keeping)

The state mandated standards require that teachers maintain a written record of student progress by maintaining proper student files with student assignments. Teachers are required to prepare daily lessons plans focused on mastering the identified curriculum objectives. Teachers are also required to use a grading system that is fair to all students and based on a set established criterion. It also necessitates that students demonstrate mastery of identified objectives through ongoing daily work assignments, projects, direct observation of performance, and test scores.

Standards of professionalism are also exhibited which include following a set schedule so that teacher responsibilities are done in a timely manner. In addition, the teacher should respond professionally to requests and instructions from the administrators.

For information on student records, see Skill 8.4.

Skill 11.2 The teacher recognizes specific practices that meet or fail to meet OCETP standards.

Based on the state-mandated performance standards, there are a list of criteria for effective teaching and performance. A teacher that meets the specific practices knows what they are and when they fall short. An example of a practice that would not meet standards would be when a teacher provides instruction and notices that the majority of the class does not comprehend the lesson and then continues on with the lesson without modifying it so that students are not confused. One of the criteria of an effective teacher is that they adjust the lesson based on monitoring.

Additional practices that meet OCETP standards include the following:
Ensuring that the instructional objectives are conveyed to the students so they know in advance what they are supposed to learn; explaining how the objectives relate to information taught in the past and how it will link to future subject matter; making sure that all of the students in the class are involved in the lesson by using appropriate questioning and guided practice; using a wide range of methods to teach the learning objectives and clearly explain how to complete an assignment; demonstrating how the required skills can be performed and monitoring the students mastery of stated goals to ensure the goals are met and implementing modifications if necessary; ensuring that students practice their newly acquired skills under direct supervision; and establishing closure to the lesson by summarizing key points and explaining the significance of what has been learned.

Skill 11.3 The teacher demonstrates knowledge of OCETP criteria for evaluating teacher skills in managing and delivering instruction.

The Oklahoma Criteria For Effective Teaching (OCETP) and Administrative Performance (70 O. S. § 6-101.10 AND § 6-101.11) has set specific indicators to evaluate the performance of teachers.

The teacher management indicators include the following:
Preparation – The teacher plans in advance how the lesson will be delivered in the immediate short term and in the long term.
Routine – the teacher does not utilize the class time for things that are not a part of the normal instructional day. The time that the student's are on task and completing the class objectives is maximized for optimal performance.
Discipline – the teacher explains in detail the behavior objectives and lets the student's know what the expectations are in the area of behavior.
Learning Environment - the teacher puts the students at ease and gains their trust making the environment conducive to learning. The class is organized, pleasant, and safe for the students.

The teacher instructional indicators include the following:
Establishes Objectives – the teacher conveys the instructional objectives appropriately to the class.
Stresses Sequence – the teacher explains how the topic being studied is related to subject matter taught in the past and provides links to things that will be studied in the future that tie in with the current topic.
Relates Objectives – the teacher relates the objectives of the lesson to things that the student is familiar with so that the lesson is relevant towards the student's interests.
Involves All learners- the teacher makes sure that everyone in the class understands the lesson and is involved and participating in the lesson. The teacher utilizes questioning techniques, signals, and guided practice to ensure that all students are involved in the lesson.

Explains Content – the teacher instructs utilizing a wide variety of methods to ensure the content of the lesson is clear to students with various learning styles.
Explains Direction - the teacher provides clear and succinct directions on lesson objectives so that everyone understands what they need to accomplish.
Monitors – the teacher checks out and reviews all of the work done to make sure that students are progressing toward stated objectives.
Adjust Based on Monitoring – after monitoring how the class is performing with a specific task the teacher will adjust how the information is being taught dependent upon the results of the monitoring.
Guides Practice - the teacher ensures that all of the students practice their newly acquired skills while being observed.
Provides for independent practice – the teacher ensures that student's practice the new skills they are being taught all by themselves.
Established closure – the teacher makes sure the lesson planned has a closing point so students are aware that the lesson is over and a synopsis of the lesson is provided.

Skill 11.4 The teacher applies OCETP criteria in reflecting on one's management and instructional practices and determining whether modifications are necessary.

The OCTEP criteria listed in skill 11.3 should be continuously utilized for self assessment purposes to determine if current teaching practices are in line with the requirements set forth.

Effective management is demonstrated by four key elements being in place that include: preparation; routine; discipline, and a learning environment. In the area of preparation, teachers should ensure that they plan to deliver the lesson with short and long-term objectives. The class routine should be structured in such a manner that no time is wasted on non-instructional routines and transitional time periods are used effectively. In the area of discipline there are clearly defined expectations of how students should behave; and the learning environment should be one in which the teacher has established a rapport with students and the atmosphere is pleasant and organized, contributing to a good learning situation.

Teachers should continuously evaluate their own performance to ensure that the standards are being achieved.

TEACHER STUDY GUIDE

Competency 0012 The teacher fosters positive interaction with school colleagues, parents/families, and organizations in the community to actively engage them in support of students' learning and well-being.

Skill 12.1 The teacher applies strategies for active collaboration with colleagues (e.g., other teachers, mentors, supervisors, special needs professionals, administrators, support staff) to address the needs of students and improve the learning environment.

Child Study Teams

Collaborative teams play a crucial role in meeting the needs of all students, and they are important step to identifying students with special needs. Under the Individuals with Disabilities Act (IDEA), which federally mandates special education services in every state, it is the responsibility of public schools to ensure consultative, evaluative and if necessary, prescriptive services to children with special needs. In most school districts, this responsibility is handled by a collaborative group of called the Child Study Team (CST). If a teacher or parent suspects a child to have academic, social or emotional problems are referred to the CST where a team consisting of educational professionals (including teachers, specialists, the school psychologist, guidance, and other support staff) review the student's case and situation through meetings with the teacher and/or parents/guardians. The CST will determine what evaluations or tests are necessary, if any, and will also assess the results. Based on these results, the CST will suggest a plan of action if one is felt necessary.

Special education teachers, resource specialists, school psychologists, and other special education staff are present on school campuses to be resources for students who have special educational needs. Occasionally, new teachers fear that when a resource specialist seeks to work with them, it means that the resource specialist does not think they are doing an adequate job in dealing with students with Individualized Education Plans (IEPs). Quite the contrary. Many IEPs require that resource specialists work in students' general education classrooms. Considering that school is more than just about the learning of content standards—that it is often about socialization and the development of citizens for a democratic society—it is both counterproductive and unfair to exclude students from regular classrooms, even if they need some individualized assistance from a special education resource teacher.

TEACHER STUDY GUIDE

Service Models for Students with Special Needs

First and foremost, teachers must be familiar with what is stated in their students' IEPs. For example, some IEPs have explicit strategies that teachers should use to help the students learn effectively. Additionally, teachers may want to provide additional attention to these students to ensure that they are progressing effectively. Sometimes, it may be necessary to reduce or modify assignments for students with disabilities. For example, if a teacher were to assign fifteen math problems for homework, for particular students, the assignment might be more effective if it is five problems for the students with disabilities. Teachers can use multiple strategies, group students in flexible situations, and pair them with others who can be of greater assistance.

Special education services are offered in many ways, and a student's IEP and CST will determine their least restrictive environment. Inclusion refers to the situation where a student with special needs remains in the regular education classroom with the support of special education support staff (usually in the form of a personal or class aid). Sometimes, a student requires some resource room, or pull out, services. In these cases, students are taken into smaller class settings where personalized services are delivered in their greatest area(s) of difficulty. Students who have difficulty functioning in a regular education classroom are placed in smaller classrooms for the full school day. These are sometimes referred to as LD, or learning disabled, classrooms.

Skill 12.2 The teacher understands schools and school systems within the context of the larger community.

In some places, the community is one entity and the school is another and rarely do the two meet. In communities where the schools are doing the best job, community members take a lot of interest in their doings and their welfare and constantly work to bring the two closer together. Continuing education courses that invite the community in to develop interests or skills they might not be able to develop otherwise have sprung up in schools all over the country. Sports teams that the community takes pride and ownership in are another way the school becomes a part of the larger community, and in some communities the school system encourages that. Often, blood drives are run out of the local school. The gyms may be the biggest meeting rooms in the city or county and can be utilized by the larger community.

In the early days of public education, teachers usually lived with one of the families in the community, and the community itself felt a strong sense of ownership in the school. As public education has become more and more organized and has involved political entities at higher levels with funding coming from more than the local source, the feeling of ownership has lost some of its vigor.

The large buildings are owned by the people and using them as resources helps everyone. It brings the community into the school and increases a sense of ownership and community pride.

Skill 12.3 The teacher applies strategies for initiating and maintaining effective communication with parents/guardians and recognizing factors that may promote communication in given circumstances.

Effective teaching and learning for students begins with teachers who can demonstrate sensitivity for diversity in teaching and relationships within school communities. Student portfolios include work that has a multicultural perspective and inclusion where students share cultural and ethnic life experiences in their learning. Teachers are responsive to including cultural and diverse resources in their curriculum and instructional practices. Exposing students to culturally sensitive room decorations and posters that show positive and inclusive messages is one way to demonstrate inclusion of multiple cultures. Teachers should also continuously make cultural connections that are relevant and empowering for all students and communicate academic and behavioral expectations. Cultural sensitivity is communicated beyond the classroom with parents and community members to establish and maintain relationships.

Other artifacts that could reflect teacher/student sensitivity to diversity might consist of the following:

- Student portfolios reflecting multicultural/multiethnic perspectives
- Journals and reflections from field trips/ guest speakers from diverse cultural backgrounds
- Printed materials and wall displays from multicultural perspectives
- Parent/guardian letters in a variety of languages reflecting cultural diversity
- Projects that include cultural history and diverse inclusions
- Disaggregated student data reflecting cultural groups
- Classroom climate of professionalism that fosters diversity and cultural inclusion

The target of diversity allows teachers a variety of opportunities to expand their experiences with students, staff, community members and parents from culturally diverse backgrounds, so that their experiences can be proactively applied in promoting cultural diversity inclusion in the classroom. Teachers are able to engage and challenge students to develop and incorporate their own diversity skills in building character and relationships with cultures beyond their own. In changing the thinking patterns of students to become more cultural inclusive in the 21st century, teachers are addressing the globalization of our world.

TEACHER STUDY GUIDE

Providing parents with opportunities to attend in-service workshops on data discussions with teachers and administrators creates additional opportunity for parents to ask questions and become actively involved in monitoring their student's educational progress. With state assessments, parents should look for the words "passed" or "met/exceeded standards" in interpreting the numerical data on student reports. Parents who maintain an active involvement in their students' education will attend school opportunities to promote their understanding of academic and educational achievement for students.

Skill 12.4 The teacher recognizes how to use community resources to enrich learning experiences

In order to create personalized learning communities, educators must use information from the school experience to create relationships that create bridges of collaboration between school and community resources. The interaction chart of personalized learning shows the research of Clarke and Frazer (2003) in evaluating the developmental needs for students in school communities:

Interactions in Personalized Learning

Personal Needs	Relationships	School Practices
Self-Expression	Recognition from school	Provides equity
Creating self-identity	Acceptance-feeling of belonging	Shared community
Choosing one's own path	Creating trust	Range of options for student development
Freedom to take risks	Respect from community	Taking responsibility
Using one's imagination to view self projections	Fulfilling one's purpose in life	Creating greater challenges
Successful mastery	Confirm one's progress and goals	Having clear expectations for performance

(as adapted from Clarke and Frazer, 2003)

In a personalized learning community, students must feel a sense of connection to teachers and staff. Teachers know students by name and individual expression. Greeting students in the morning with names and a special recognition such as, "Jamie, thanks for participating the school's recycling program," or "Great job, David, in that last quarter touchdown at last Friday's football game," will go a long way in creating an affirming and connected school environment.

OPTE

TEACHER STUDY GUIDE

Teachers who take the time to get to know students will find that developing student learning plans for academic performance is an easier task when communication about testing data is shared and evaluated with the student. Students can share if they were truly engaged in taking the pre-assessment for an Algebra class or simply filling in the blanks due to a falling out with a friend during the period that preceded your math class. Having authentic communication can help facilitate authentic assessment that can help both teacher and student create clear expectations for academic and behavioral performances in classrooms.

Students who feel like they belong in their school communities may feel more motivated to succeed academically than students who simply feel like a number among the thousands of students. Parents and community members who are actively involved in PTSAs and community after school support groups will find that students actually appreciate having their support and involvement in school activities and governance.

Community support provides additional resources for classrooms and school communities on limited District budgets. Additional grant sources from local PTSAs and educational organizations continue to provide financial resources for teachers seeking to provide maximal learning opportunities for students.

See also Skill 9.2.

Competency 0013 The teacher understands the legal aspects of teaching, including the rights of students and parents/families, as well as the legal rights and responsibilities of the teacher.

Skill 13.1 The teacher applies knowledge of teachers' legal rights and responsibilities (e.g., with regard to student discipline, situations involving suspected child abuse, the expression of political views).

Teachers are legally required to make sure that all students under their care are safe from harm. This entails anticipating probable dangers and taking the necessary steps to protect students from harm.

The First and Fourteenth Amendments to the U.S. Constitution prevent civil authorities from instituting any law that confers preference to a specific religion or gets in the way of the free expression of religious beliefs. Court rulings interpreting this prohibition have indicated that comparative religion and the history of religion may be studied in the public schools, as long as the lessons do not attempt to promote a specific religious ideology. In order to adhere to constitutional legislation, teachers should present religious information from a historical or cultural standpoint.

Teachers have the first amendment right of freedom of speech. Their rights are greatest when they are far away from school, but they maintain some rights in school. In school, administrative authorities have the broad, general discretion to regulate the content, manner and ambiance in which education takes place.

A school committee could regulate a teacher's classroom speech if the regulation is reasonably related to a legitimate educational interest; and the school provided the teacher with notice of what conduct was prohibited. Retaliation against a teacher for in-class speech is not permitted unless the teacher had been informed of the prohibitions based on existing regulations.

Teachers also have a right to express themselves as citizens about matters of public concern. Teachers may be dismissed for immorality, willful neglect of duty, cruelty, incompetency, teaching disloyalty to the U. S. government, moral turpitude, or criminal sexual activity.

TEACHER STUDY GUIDE

Abuse Situations

The child who is undergoing the abuse is the one whose needs must be served first. A suspected case gone unreported may destroy a child's life, and their subsequent life as a functional adult. It is the duty of any citizen who suspects abuse and neglect to make a report, and it is especially important and required for State licensed and certified persons to make a report. All reports can be kept confidential if required, but it is best to disclose your identity in case more information is required of you. This is a personal matter that has no impact on qualifications for license or certification. Failure to make a report when abuse or neglect is suspected is punishable by revocation of certification and license, a fine, and criminal charges.

It is the right of any accused individual to have counsel and make a defense, as in any matter of law. The procedure for reporting makes clear the rights of the accused, who stands before the court innocent until proven guilty, with the right to representation, redress and appeal, as in all matters of United States law. The State is cautious about receiving spurious reports, but investigates any that seem real enough. Some breaches of standards of decency are not reportable offenses, such as possession of pornography that is not hidden from children. But go ahead and make the report and let the counselor make the decision. Your conscience is clear, and you have followed all procedures that keep you from liability. Your obligation to report is immediate when you suspect abuse.

There is no time given as an acceptable or safe period of time to wait before reporting, so hesitation to report may be a cause for action against you. Do not wait once your suspicion is firm. All you need to have is a reasonable suspicion, not actual proof, which is the job for the investigators.

Many safe and helpful interventions are available to the classroom teacher when dealing with a student who is suffering serious emotional disturbances. First, and foremost, the teacher must maintain open communication with the parents and other professionals who are involved with the student whenever overt behavior characteristics are exhibited. Students with behavior disorders need constant behavior modification, which may involve two-way communication between the home and school on a daily basis.

The teacher must establish an environment that promotes appropriate behavior for all students as well as respect for one another. The students may need to be informed of any special needs that their classmates may have so they can give due consideration. The teacher should also initiate a behavior modification program for any student that might show emotional or behavioral disorders. Such behavior modification plans can be effective means of preventing deviant behavior. If deviant behavior does occur, the teacher should have arranged for a safe and secure time-out place where the student can go for a respite and an opportunity to regain self-control.

OPTE

Often when a behavior disorder is more severe, the student must be involved in a more concentrated program aimed at alleviating deviant behavior such as psychotherapy. In such instances, the school psychologist, guidance counselor, or behavior specialist is directly involved with the student and provides counseling and therapy on a regular basis. Frequently they are also involved with the student's family.

As a last resort, many families are turning to drug therapy. Once viewed as a radical step, administering drugs to children to balance their emotions or control their behavior has become a widely used form of therapy. Of course, only a medical doctor can prescribe such drugs. Great care must be exercised when giving pills to children in order to change their behavior, especially since so many medicines have undesirable side effects. It is important to know that these drugs relieve only the symptoms of behavior and do not get at the underlying causes. Parents and teachers need to be educated as to the side effects of these medications.

Skill 13.2 The teacher understands laws related to students' rights (e.g., assuring equal access to education, providing an appropriate education for students with special needs, maintaining confidentiality, ensuring due process)

One of the first things that a teacher learns is how to obtain resources and help for his/her students. All schools have guidelines for receiving this assistance especially since the implementation of the Americans with Disabilities Act. The first step in securing help is for the teacher to approach the school's administration or exceptional education department for direction in attaining special services or resources for qualifying students. Many schools have a committee designated for addressing these needs such as a Child Study Team or Core Team. These teams are made up of both regular and exceptional education teachers, school psychologists, guidance counselors, and administrators. The particular student's classroom teacher usually has to complete some initial paper work and will need to do some behavioral observations.

The teacher will take this information to the appropriate committee for discussion and consideration. The committee will recommend the next step to be taken. Often subsequent steps include a complete psychological evaluation along with certain physical examinations such as vision and hearing screening and a complete medical examination by a doctor.

The referral of students for this process is usually relatively simple for the classroom teacher and requires little more than some initial paper work and discussion. The services and resources the student receives as a result of the process typically prove to be invaluable to the student with behavioral disorders.

At times, the teacher must go beyond the school system to meet the needs of some students. An awareness of special services and resources and how to obtain them is essential to all teachers and their students. When the school system is unable to address the needs of a student, the teacher often must take the initiative and contact agencies within the community. Frequently there is no special policy for finding resources. It is simply up to the individual teacher to be creative and resourceful and to find whatever help the student needs. Meeting the needs of all students is certainly a team effort that is most often spearheaded by the classroom teacher.

There is a saying, "If you're going to be an alcoholic or drug addict in America, you will be." Cynical but true, this comment implies exposure to alcohol and drugs is 100%. We now have a wide-spread second generation of drug abusers in families. And alcohol is the oldest drug of abuse known to humankind, with many families affected for three and four or more known generations. It's hard to tell youth to eschew drugs when Mom and Dad, who grew up in the early illicit drug era, have a little toot or smoke and a few drinks on the weekends, or more often. Educators, therefore, are not only likely to, but often do face students who are high on something in school. Of course, they are not only a hazard to their own safety and those of others, but their ability to be productive learners is greatly diminished, if not non-existent. They show up instead of skip, because it's not always easy or practical for them to spend the day away from home, but not in school. Unless they can stay inside they are at risk of being picked up for truancy. Some enjoy being high in school, getting a sense of satisfaction by putting something over on the system. Some just don't take drug use seriously enough to think usage at school might be inappropriate.

Family involvement

Under the IDEA, parent/guardian involvement in the development of the student's IEP is required and absolutely essential for the advocacy of the disabled student's educational needs. IEPs must be tailored to meet the student's needs, and no one knows those needs better than the parent/guardian and other significant family members. Optimal conditions for a disabled student's education exist when teachers, school administrators, special education professionals and parents/guardians work together to design and execute the IEP.

Due process

Under the IDEA, Congress provides safeguards for students against schools' actions, including the right to sue in court, and encourages states to develop hearing and mediation systems to resolve disputes. No student or their parents/guardians can be denied due process because of disability.

TEACHER STUDY GUIDE

Inclusion, mainstreaming, and least restrictive environment

Inclusion, mainstreaming and least restrictive environment are interrelated policies under the IDEA, with varying degrees of statutory imperatives.

- Inclusion is the right of students with disabilities to be placed in the regular classroom.
- Lease restrictive environment is the mandate that children be educated to the maximum extent appropriate with their non-disabled peers.
- Mainstreaming is a policy where disabled students can be placed in the regular classroom, as long as such placement does not interfere with the student's educational plan.

Confidentiality

It is illegal for teachers to disclose any information concerning any child acquired by them in their role as a teacher, except that which is required in the performance of contractual duties. The exception to this would be in the case of a parent or guardian of the child who is entitled to receive the information upon request. School districts are allowed to give information about students who participate in athletic and school activities, and those who are awarded honors or commendations. Information about age and academic records may be given to proper school and college officials at the discretion of the Board of Education.

Skill 13.3 The teacher applies knowledge of the rights and responsibilities of parents/guardians in various situations (e.g., in relation to student records, school attendance).

The teacher is responsible for conveying to parents and guardians the importance of education and regular attendance in school. It is illegal for a parent or guardian of a child between the ages of 5 and 18 to neglect or refuse to compel their child to attend school and follow the rules of some public, private or other school, unless alternative education is provided for the full term the schools of the district are in session or the child is excused.

The child will be excused if they cannot attend school due to a mental or physical disability that is certified by a licensed and practicing doctor. They will also be excused from attending school if there is an emergency. Students age 16 and over may be excused from attending school if they have the joint agreement of the school administrator and the parent or guardian, unless it is determined that leaving school is not in the best interest of the child or the community. A school district can excuse a student from attending school for the purpose of observing religious holy days if before the absence, the parent or guardian, turns in a written request for the excused absence.

The attendance officer is required to make sure the attendance requirements are adhered to. If a parent or guardian, or child violates the attendance laws, they will be guilty of a misdemeanor and have to pay a fine.

TEACHER STUDY GUIDE

The principal of the school is required to keep a full and complete record of the attendance of all children at each school. They should advise the attendance officer in the district of any absences and the reason for the absence. The parent or guardian is required to advise the child's teacher of the reason for any absences. The principal is also required to advise the parent or guardian of any absences for any part of the school day.

The attendance officer and teacher are required to report to the school health officer all absences due to illness. The attendance officer should, if justified by the circumstances, promptly give the parent who has not complied with these provisions oral and documented or written warning to the last-known address of the student. Within 5 days of the warning having been received, the parent or guardian is required to comply with the attendance regulations. If the parents do not comply, the attendance officer can file a complaint against the parent if the child is absent without valid excuse for 4 or more days or parts of days within a four week time frame, or without valid excuse for 10 or more days within a semester, then the attendance officer should advise the parent immediately and report the absences to the district attorney for juvenile proceedings pursuant to Title 10 of the Oklahoma Statutes.

For information regarding student records, see Skill 5.4.

TEACHER STUDY GUIDE

Sample Test

Directions: Read each item and select the best response.

1. **What are critical elements of instructional process?**

   A. Content, goals, teacher needs

   B. Means of getting money to regulate instruction

   C. Content, materials, activities, goals, learner needs

   D. Materials, definitions, assignments

2. **What would improve planning for instruction?**

   A. Describe the role of the teacher and student

   B. Evaluate the outcomes of instruction

   C. Rearrange the order of activities

   D. Give outside assignments

3. **When are students more likely to understand complex ideas?**

   A. If they do outside research before coming to class

   B. Later when they write out the definitions of complex words

   C. When they attend a lecture on the subject

   D. When they are clearly defined by the teacher and are given examples and non-examples of the concept

4. **What is one component of the instructional planning model that must be given careful evaluation?**

   A. Students' prior knowledge and skills

   B. The script the teacher will use in instruction

   C. Future lesson plans

   D. Parent participation

5. **When is utilization of instructional materials most effective?**

    A. When the activities are sequenced

    B. When the materials are prepared ahead of time

    C. When the students choose the pages to work on

    D. When the students create the instructional materials

6. **What should a teacher do when students have not responded well to an instructional activity?**

    A. Reevaluate learner needs

    B. Request administrative help

    C. Continue with the activity another day

    D. Assign homework on the concept

7. **How can student misconduct be redirected at times?**

    A. The teacher threatens the students

    B. The teacher assigns detention to the whole class

    C. The teacher stops the activity and stares at the students

    D. The teacher effectively handles changing from one activity to another

8. **What is one way of effectively managing student conduct?**

    A. State expectations about behavior

    B. Let students discipline their peers

    C. Let minor infractions of the rules go unnoticed

    D. Increase disapproving remarks

9. **Which of the following increases appropriate behavior more than 80%?**

    A. Monitoring the halls

    B. Having class rules

    C. Having class rules, giving feedback, and having individual consequences

    D. Having class rules, and giving feedback

TEACHER STUDY GUIDE

10. **What developmental patterns should a professional teacher assess to meet the needs of the student?**

    A. Academic, regional, and family background

    B. Social, physical, academic

    C. Academic, physical, and family background

    D. Physical, family, ethnic background

11. **According to Piaget, what stage is characterized by the ability to think abstractly and to use logic?**

    A. Concrete operations

    B. Pre-operational

    C. Formal operations

    D. Conservative operational

12. **At approximately what age is the average child able to define abstract terms such as honesty and justice?**

    A. 10-12 years old

    B. 4-6 years old

    C. 14-16 years old

    D. 6-8 years old

13. **Johnny, a middle-schooler, comes to class, uncharacteristically tired, distracted, withdrawn, sullen, and cries easily. What would be the teacher's first response?**

    A. Send him to the office to sit

    B. Call his parents

    C. Ask him what is wrong

    D. Ignore his behavior

14. **Sam, a 10-year-old fifth grader, has suddenly started to stutter when speaking. What is the most likely speech problem?**

    A. A genetic defect

    B. A new habit

    C. Evidence of an emotional conflict

    D. An attention-getting device

TEACHER STUDY GUIDE

15. **Andy shows up to class abusive and irritable. He is often late, sleeps in class, sometimes slurs his speech, and has an odor of drinking. What is the first intervention to take?**

    A. Confront him, relying on a trusting relationship you think you have

    B. Do a lesson on alcohol abuse, making an example of him.

    C. Do nothing, it is better to err on the side of failing to identify substance abuse

    D. Call administration, avoid conflict, and supervise others carefully.

16. **A 16 year-old girl who has been looking sad writes an essay in which the main protagonist commits suicide. You overhear her talking about suicide. What do you do?**

    A. Report this immediately to school administration, talk to the girl, letting her know you will talk to her parents about it

    B. Report this immediately to authorities

    C. Report this immediately to school administration. Make your own report to authorities if required by protocol in your school. Do nothing else

    D. Just give the child some extra attention, as it may just be that's all she's looking for

OPTE

17. **You are leading a substance abuse discussion for health class. The students present their belief that marijuana is not harmful to their health. What set of data would refute their claim?**

   A. It is more carcinogenic than nicotine, lowers resistance to infection, worsens acne, and damages brain cells

   B. it damages brain cells, causes behavior changes in prenatally exposed infants, leads to other drug abuse, and causes short-term memory loss

   C. it lowers tolerance for frustration, causes eye damage, increases paranoia, and lowers resistance to infection

   D. It leads to abusing alcohol, lowers white blood cell count, reduces fertility, and causes gout

18. **Jeanne, a bright, attentive student is in first hour English. She is quiet, but very alert, often visually scanning the room in random patterns. Her pupils are dilated and she has a slight but noticeable tremor in her hands. She fails to note a cue given from her teacher. At odd moments she will act as if responding to stimuli that aren't there by suddenly changing her gaze. When spoken to directly, she has a limited response, but her teacher has a sense she is not herself. What should the teacher do?**

   A. Ask the student if she is all right, then let it go, as there are not enough signals to be alarmed

   B. Meet with the student after class to get more information before making a referral

   C. Send the student to the office to see the health nurse

   D. Quietly call for administration, remain calm and be careful not to alarm the class

TEACHER STUDY GUIDE

19. **Marcus is a first grade boy of good developmental attainment. His learning progress is good the first half of the year. He shows no indicators of emotional distress. After the holiday break, he returns much changed. He is quieter, sullen even, tending to play alone. He has moments of tearfulness, sometimes almost without cause. He avoids contact with adults as often as he can. Even play with his friends has become limited. He has episodes of wetting not seen before, and often wants to sleep in school. What approach is appropriate for this sudden change in behavior?**

   A. Give him some time to adjust. The holiday break was probably too much fun to come back to school from

   B. Report this change immediately to administration. Do not call the parents until administration decides a course of action

   C. Document his daily behavior carefully as soon as you notice such a change, report to administration the next month or so in a meeting

   D. Make a courtesy call to the parents to let them know he is not acting like himself, being sure to tell them he is not making trouble for others

20. **What have recent studies regarding effective teachers concluded?**

   A. Effective teachers let students establish rules

   B. Effective teachers establish routines by the sixth week of school

   C. Effective teachers state their own policies and establish consistent class rules and procedures on the first day of class

   D. Effective teachers establish flexible routines

21. **To maintain the flow of events in the classroom, what should an effective teacher do?**

   A. Work only in small groups

   B. Use only whole class activities

   C. Direct attention to content, rather than focusing the class on misbehavior

   D. Follow lectures with written assignments

OPTE

TEACHER STUDY GUIDE

22. **Why is it important for a teacher to pose a question before calling on students to answer?**

    A. It helps manage student conduct

    B. It keeps the students as a group focused on the class work

    C. It allows students time to collaborate

    D. It gives the teacher time to walk among the students

23. **Which statement is an example of specific praise?**

    A. "John, you are the only person in class not paying attention"

    B. "William, I thought we agreed that you would turn in all of your homework"

    C. "Robert, you did a good job staying in line. See how it helped us get to music class on time"

    D. "Class, you did a great job cleaning up the art room"

24. **What is one way a teacher can supplement verbal praise?**

    A. Help students evaluate their own performance and supply self-reinforcement

    B. Give verbal praise more frequently

    C. Give tangible rewards such as stickers or treats

    D. Have students practice giving verbal praise

25. **Reducing off task time and maximizing the amount of time students spend attending to academic tasks is closely related to which of the following?**

    A. Using whole class instruction only

    B. Business-like behaviors of the teacher

    C. Dealing only with major teaching functions

    D. Giving students a maximum of two minutes to come to order

OPTE

26. **The concept of efficient use of time includes which of the following?**

    A. Daily review, seatwork, and recitation of concepts

    B. Lesson initiation, transition, and comprehension check

    C. Review, test, review

    D. Punctuality, management transition, and wait time avoidance

27. **What steps are important in the review of subject matter in the classroom?**

    A. A lesson-initiating review, topic and a lesson-end review

    B. A preview of the subject matter, an in-depth discussion, and a lesson-end review

    C. A rehearsal of the subject matter and a topic summary within the lesson

    D. A short paragraph synopsis of the previous days lesson and a written review at the end of the lesson

28. **What is a sample of an academic transition signal?**

    A. "How do clouds form?"

    B. "Today we are going to study clouds."

    C. "We have completed today's lesson."

    D. "That completes the description of cumulus clouds. Now we will look at the description of cirrus clouds."

29. **What is an example of a low order question?**

    A. "Why is it important to recycle items in your home"

    B. "Compare how glass and plastics are recycled"

    C. "What items do we recycle in our county"

    D. "Explain the importance of recycling in our county"

30. **The teacher states that the lesson the students will be engaged in will consist of a review of the material from the previous day, demonstration of the scientific of an electronic circuit, and small group work on setting up an electronic circuit. What has the teacher demonstrated?**

    A. The importance of reviewing

    B. Giving the general framework for the lesson to facilitate learning

    C. Giving students the opportunity to leave if they are not interested in the lesson

    D. Providing momentum for the lesson

31. **Wait-time has what effect?**

    A. Gives structure to the class discourse

    B. Fewer chain and low level questions are asked with more higher-level questions included

    C. Gives the students time to evaluate the response

    D. Gives the opportunity for in-depth discussion about the topic

32. **What is one benefit of amplifying a student's response?**

    A. It helps the student develop a positive self-image

    B. It is helpful to other students who are in the process of learning the reasoning or steps in answering the question

    C. It allows the teacher to cover more content

    D. It helps to keep the information organized

33. **A study by Darch and Gersten that examined the effects of positive feedback on the reading performance of seven and eight-year old learning disabled students found which result?**

    A. Students exhibited more self-esteem

    B. Students exhibited more on-task behavior

    C. Students were willing to answer more questions

    D. Students worked better in small groups

34. **When is optimal benefit reached when handling an incorrect student response?**

    A. When specific praise is used

    B. When the other students are allowed to correct that student

    C. When the student is redirected to a better problem solving approach

    D. When the teacher asks simple questions, provides cues to clarify, or gives assistance for working out the correct response

35. **What are the two ways concepts can be taught?**

    A. Factually and interpretively

    B. Inductively and deductively

    C. Conceptually and inductively

    D. Analytically and facilitatively

36. **Using pro-active expressions and repetition has what effect on students?**

    A. Helps student become aware of important elements of content

    B. Helps students develop positive self-esteem

    C. Helps students tolerate the lecture format of instruction

    D. Helps students to complete homework correctly

37. **How can the teacher help students become more work oriented and less disruptive?**

    A. Seek their input for content instruction

    B. Challenge the students with a task and show genuine enthusiasm for it

    C. Use behavior modification techniques with all students

    D. Make sure lesson plans are complete for the week

38. **What is an effective way to prepare students for testing?**

    A. Minimize the importance of the test

    B. Orient the students to the test, telling them of the purpose, how the results will be used and how it is relevant to them

    C. Use the same format for every test are given

    D. Have them construct an outline to study from

39. **How will students have a fair chance to demonstrate what they know on a test?**

    A. The examiner has strictly enforced rules for taking the test

    B. The examiner provides a comfortable setting free of distractions and positively encourages the students

    C. The examiner provides frequent stretch breaks to the students

    D. The examiner stresses the importance of the test to the overall grade

40. **What is an example of formative feedback?**

    A. The results of an intelligence test

    B. Correcting the tests in small groups

    C. Verbal behavior that expresses approval of a student response to a test item

    D. Scheduling a discussion prior to the test

41. **How could a KWL chart be used in instruction?**

    A. To motivate students to do a research paper

    B. To assess prior knowledge of the students

    C. To assist in teaching skills

    D. To put events in sequential order

42. **How can the teacher establish a positive climate in the classroom?**

    A. Help students see the unique contributions of individual differences

    B. Use whole group instruction for all content areas

    C. Help students divide into cooperative groups based on ability

    D. Eliminate teaching strategies that allow students to make choices

43. **How can students use a computer desktop publishing center?**

    A. To set up a classroom budget

    B. To create student made books

    C. To design a research project

    D. To create a classroom behavior management system

44. **Which of the following is an example of a synthesis question according to Bloom's taxonomy?**

    A. "What is the definition of _____?"

    B. "Compare _____ to _____."

    C. "Match column A to column B."

    D. "Propose an alternative to _____."

45. **What is a good strategy for teaching ethnically diverse students?**

    A. Don't focus on the students' culture

    B. Expect them to assimilate easily into your classroom

    C. Imitate their speech patterns

    D. Include ethnic studies in the curriculum

46. **How many stages of intellectual development does Piaget define?**

    A. Two

    B. Four

    C. Six

    D. Eight

47. **What is the most significant development emerging in children at age two?**

    A. Immune system develops

    B. Socialization occurs

    C. Language develops

    D. Perception develops

48. **According to Piaget, when does the development of symbolic functioning and language take place?**

    A. Concrete operations stage

    B. Formal operations stage

    C. Sensorimotor stage

    D. Preoperational stage

49. **What is the learning theorist's view of language acquisition?**

    A. Language is shaped by the reinforcement children receive from their caretakers

    B. Language is the result of innate biological mechanisms

    C. Language results spontaneously

    D. Language is developed through systematic instruction

50. **Bobby, a nine year-old, has been caught stealing frequently in the classroom. What might be a factor contributing to this behavior?**

    A. Need for the items stolen

    B. Serious emotional disturbance

    C. Desire to experiment

    D. A normal stage of development

51. **What does the validity of a test refer to?**

    A. Its consistency

    B. Its usefulness

    C. Its accuracy

    D. The degree of true scores it provides

52. **What is the best definition for an achievement test?**

    A. It measures mechanical and practical abilities

    B. It measures broad areas of knowledge that are the result of cumulative learning experiences

    C. It measures the ability to learn to perform a task

    D. It measures performance related to specific, recently acquired information

53. **Which of the following is an accurate description of ESL students?**

    A. Remedial students

    B. Exceptional education students

    C. Are not a homogeneous group

    D. Feel confident in communicating in English when with their peers

54. What is an effective way to help a non-English speaking student succeed in class?

    A. Refer the child to a specialist

    B. Maintain an encouraging, success-oriented atmosphere

    C. Help them assimilate by making them use English exclusively

    D. Help them cope with the content materials you presently use

55. What should be considered when evaluating textbooks for content?

    A. Type of print used

    B. Number of photos used

    C. Free of cultural stereotyping

    D. Outlines at the beginning of each chapter

56. How can text be modified for low-level ESL students?

    A. Add visuals and illustrations

    B. Let students write definitions

    C. Change text to a narrative form

    D. Have students write details out from the text

57. Which of the following is considered a study skill?

    A. Using graphs, tables, and maps

    B. Using a desk-top publishing program

    C. Explaining important vocabulary words

    D. Asking for clarification

58. When using a kinesthetic approach, what would be an appropriate activity?

    A. List

    B. Match

    C. Define

    D. Debate

59. Etienne is an ESL student. He has begun to engage in conversation which produces a connected narrative. What developmental stage for second language acquisition is he in?

    A. Early production

    B. Speech emergence

    C. Preproduction

    D. Intermediate fluency

60. **What is a roadblock to second language learning?**

    A. Students are forced to speak

    B. Students speak only when ready

    C. Mistakes are considered a part of learning

    D. The focus is on oral communication

61. **What do cooperative learning methods all have in common?**

    A. Philosophy

    B. Cooperative task/cooperative reward structures

    C. Student roles and communication

    D. Teacher roles

62. **Who developed the theory of multiple intelligences?**

    A. Bruner

    B. Gardner

    C. Kagan

    D. Cooper

63. **According to research, what can be a result of specific teacher actions on behavior?**

    A. Increase in student misconduct

    B. Increase in the number of referrals

    C. Decrease in student participation

    D. Decrease in student retentions

64. **What is the definition of proactive classroom management?**

    A. Management that is constantly changing

    B. Management that is downplayed

    C. Management that gives clear and explicit instructions and rewarding compliance

    D. Management that is designed by the students

65. **What might be a result if the teacher is distracted by some unrelated event in the instruction?**

    A. Students will leave the class

    B. Students will understand the importance of class rules

    C. Students will stay on-task longer

    D. Students will lose the momentum of the lesson

66. **Why is praise for compliance important in classroom management?**

    A. Students will continue deviant behavior

    B. Desirable conduct will be repeated

    C. It reflects simplicity and warmth

    D. Students will fulfill obligations

67. **What is an effective amount of "wait time"?**

    A. 1 second

    B. 5 seconds

    C. 15 seconds

    D. 10 seconds

68. **Mr. Perez has the pictures and maps ready for his lesson. The movie is set up to go, and he tested the operation of the machine before the class came in. What is this an example of?**

    A. Controlled interruptions

    B. Housekeeping

    C. Punctuality

    D. Management transition

69. **How are standardized tests useful in assessment?**

    A. For teacher evaluation

    B. For evaluation of the administration

    C. For comparison from school to school

    D. For comparison to the population on which the test was normed

70. **Ms. Smith says, "Yes, exactly what do you mean by "It was the author's intention to mislead you." What does this illustrate?**

    A. Digression

    B. Restates response

    C. Probes a response

    D. Amplifies a response

71. **What is perhaps the most controversial issue in developmental psychology?**

    A. Interactionism

    B. Nature vs. nurture

    C. Relevance of IQ scores

    D. Change vs. external events

72. **A child exhibits the following symptoms: a lack of emotional responsivity, indifference to physical contact, abnormal social play, and abnormal speech. What is the likely diagnosis for this child?**

    A. Separation anxiety

    B. Mental retardation

    C. Autism

    D. Hypochondria

73. **What is not a way that teachers show acceptance and give value to a student response?**

    A. Acknowledging

    B. Correcting

    C. Discussing

    D. Amplifying

74. **What is teacher withitness?**

    A. Having adequate knowledge of subject matter

    B. A skill that must be mastered to attain certification

    C. Understanding the current fads and trends that affect students

    D. Attending to two tasks at once

75. **What should the teacher do when a student is tapping a pencil on the desk during a lecture?**

    A. Stop the lesson and correct the student as an example to other students

    B. Walk over to the student and quietly touch the pencil as a signal for the student to stop

    C. Announce to the class that everyone should remember to remain quiet during the lecture

    D. Ignore the student, hoping he or she will stop

Answer Key

1.	C	41.	B
2.	B	42.	A
3.	D	43.	B
4.	A	44.	D
5.	A	45.	D
6.	A	46.	B
7.	D	47.	C
8.	A	48.	D
9.	C	49.	A
10.	B	50.	B
11.	C	51.	B
12.	A	52.	B
13.	C	53.	C
14.	C	54.	B
15.	D	55.	C
16.	C	56.	A
17.	B	57.	A
18.	D	58.	B
19.	B	59.	D
20.	C	60.	A
21.	C	61.	B
22.	B	62.	B
23.	C	63.	A
24.	A	64.	C
25.	B	65.	D
26.	D	66.	B
27.	A	67.	B
28.	D	68.	B
29.	C	69.	D
30.	B	70.	C
31.	B	71.	B
32.	B	72.	C
33.	B	73.	B
34.	C	74.	D
35.	B	75.	B
36.	A		
37.	B		

TEACHER STUDY GUIDE

Rationales for Sample Questions

1. What are critical elements of instructional process? The correct answer is C: Content, materials, activities, goals, learner needs.

Goal-setting is a vital component of the instructional process. The teacher will, of course, have overall goals for her class, both short-term and long-term. However, perhaps even more important than that is the setting of goals that take into account the individual learner's needs, background, and stage of development. Making an educational program child-centered involves building on the natural curiosity children bring to school, and asking children what they want to learn. Student-centered classrooms contain not only textbooks, workbooks, and literature but also rely heavily on a variety of audiovisual equipment and computers. There are tape recorders, language masters, filmstrip projectors, and laser disc players to help meet the learning styles of the students. Planning for instructional activities entails identification or selection of the activities the teacher and students will engage in during a period of instruction.

2. What would improve planning for instruction? The correct answer is B: Evaluate the outcomes of
instruction.

Important as it is to plan content, materials, activities, goals taking into account learner needs and to base what goes on in the classroom on the results of that planning, it makes no difference if students are not able to demonstrate improvement in the skills being taught. An important part of the planning process is for the teacher to constantly adapt all aspects of the curriculum to what is actually happening in the classroom. Planning frequently misses the mark or fails to allow for unexpected factors. Evaluating the outcomes of instruction regularly and making adjustments accordingly will have a positive impact on the overall success of a teaching methodology.

3. When are students more likely to understand complex ideas? The correct answer is D: When they are clearly defined by the teacher and are given examples and nonexamples of the concept.

Several studies have been carried out to determine the effectiveness of giving examples as well as the difference in effectiveness of various types of examples. It was found conclusively that the most effective method of concept presentation included giving a definition along with examples and non-examples and also providing an explanation of them. These same studies indicate that boring examples were just as effective as interesting examples in promoting learning. Additional studies have been conducted to determine the most effective number of examples that will result in maximum student learning. These studies concluded that a few thoughtfully selected examples are just as effective as many examples. It was determined that the actual number of examples necessary to promote student learning was relative to the learning characteristics of the learners. It was again ascertained that learning is facilitated when examples are provided along with the definition.

OPTE

TEACHER STUDY GUIDE

4. What is one component of the instructional planning model that must be given careful evaluation? The answer is A. Students' prior knowledge and skills.

The teacher will, of course, have certain expectations regarding where the students will be physically and intellectually when he/she plans for a new class. However, there will be wide variations in the actual classroom. If he/she doesn't make the extra effort to understand where there are deficiencies and where there are strengths in the individual students, the planning will probably miss the mark, at least for some members of the class. This can be obtained through a review of student records, by observation, and by testing.

5. When is utilization of instructional materials most effective? The answer is A: When the activities are sequenced.

Most assignments will require more than one educational principle. It is helpful to explain to students the proper order in which these principles must be applied to complete the assignment successfully. Subsequently, students should also be informed of the nature of the assignment (i.e., cooperative learning, group project, individual assignment, etc). This is often done at the start of the assignment.

6. What should a teacher do when students have not responded well to an instructional activity? The correct answer is A: Reevaluate learner needs.

The value of teacher observations cannot be underestimated. It is through the use of observations that the teacher is able to informally assess the needs of the students during instruction. These observations will drive the lesson and determine the direction that the lesson will take based on student activity and behavior. After a lesson is carefully planned, teacher observation is the single most important component of an instructional presentation. If the teacher observes that a particular student is not on-task, she will change the method of instruction accordingly. She may change from a teacher-directed approach to a more interactive approach. Questioning will increase in order to increase the participation of the students. If appropriate, the teacher will introduce manipulative materials to the lesson. In addition, teachers may switch to a cooperative group activity, thereby removing the responsibility of instruction from the teacher and putting it on the students.

TEACHER STUDY GUIDE

7. How can student misconduct be redirected at times? The answer is D: The teacher effectively handles changing from one activity to another.
Appropriate verbal techniques include a soft non-threatening voice void of undue roughness, anger, or impatience regardless of whether the teacher is instructing, providing student alerts, or giving a behavior reprimand. Verbal techniques that may be effective in modifying student behavior, include simply stating the student's name, explaining briefly and succinctly what the student is doing that is inappropriate and what the student should be doing. Verbal techniques for reinforcing behavior include both encouragement and praise delivered by the teacher. In addition, for verbal techniques to positively affect student behavior and learning, the teacher must give clear, concise directives while implying her warmth toward the students.

8. What is one way of effectively managing student conduct? .The correct answer is A: State expectations about behavior.
The effective teacher demonstrates awareness of what the entire class is doing and is in control of the behavior of all students even when the teacher is working with only a small group of the children. In an attempt to prevent student misbehaviors the teacher makes clear, concise statements about what is happening in the classroom directing attention to content and the students' accountability for their work rather than focusing the class on the misbehavior. It is also effective for the teacher to make a positive statement about the appropriate behavior that is observed. If deviant behavior does occur, the effective teacher will specify who the deviant is, what he or she is doing wrong, and why this is unacceptable conduct or what the proper conduct would be. This can be a difficult task to accomplish as the teacher must maintain academic focus and flow while addressing and desisting misbehavior. The teacher must make clear, brief statements about the expectations without raising his/her voice and without disrupting instruction.

9. Which of the following increases appropriate behavior more than 80%? The answer is C: Having class rules, giving feedback, and having individual consequences.
Clear, consistent class rules go a long way to preventing inappropriate behavior. Effective teachers give immediate feedback to students regarding their behavior or misbehavior. If there are consequences, they should be as close as possible to the outside world, especially for adolescents. Consistency, especially with adolescents, reduces the occurrence of power struggles and teaches them that predictable consequences follow for their choice of actions.

OPTE

TEACHER STUDY GUIDE

10. What developmental patterns should a professional teacher assess to meet the needs of the student? The correct answer is B: Social, physical, academic.

The effective teacher applies knowledge of physical, social, and academic developmental patterns and of individual differences, to meet the instructional needs of all students in the classroom and. The most important premise of child development is that all domains of development (physical, social, and academic) are integrated. The teacher has a broad knowledge and thorough understanding of the development that typically occurs during the students' current period of life. More importantly, the teacher understands how children learn best during each period of development. An examination of the student's file coupled with ongoing evaluation assures a successful educational experience for both teacher and students.

11. According to Piaget, what stage is characterized by the ability to think abstractly and to use logic? The correct answer is C: Formal operations.

The four development stages are described in Piaget's theory as follows:
1. Sensorimotor stage: from birth to age 2 years (children experience the world through movement and senses).
2. Preoperational stage: from ages 2 to 7 (acquisition of motor skills).
3. Concrete operational stage: from ages 7 to 11 (children begin to think logically about concrete events).
4. Formal operational stage: after age 11 (development of abstract reasoning).

These chronological periods are approximate and, in light of the fact that studies have demonstrated great variation between children, cannot be seen as rigid norms. Furthermore, these stages occur at different ages, depending upon the domain of knowledge under consideration. The ages normally given for the stages reflect when each stage tends to predominate even though one might elicit examples of two, three, or even all four stages of thinking at the same time from one individual, depending upon the domain of knowledge and the means used to elicit it.

12. At approximately what age is the average child able to define abstract terms such as honesty and justice? The answer is A: 10-12 years old.

The usual age for the fourth stage (the formal operational stage) as described by Piaget is from 10 to 12 years old. It is in this stage that children begin to be able to define abstract terms.

OPTE

TEACHER STUDY GUIDE

13. Johnny, a middle-schooler, comes to class uncharacteristically tired, distracted, withdrawn, sullen, and cries easily. What would be the teacher's first response? The answer is C: Ask him what is wrong.
If a teacher has developed a trusting relationship with a child, the reasons for the child's behavior may come out. It might be that the child needs to tell someone what is going on and is seeking a confidant, and a trusted teacher can intervene. If the child is unwilling to talk to the teacher about what is going on, the next step is to contact the parents, who may or may not be willing to explain why the child is the way he/she is. If they simply do not know, then it's time to add a professional physician or counselor to the mix.

14. Sam, a 10-year-old fifth grader, has suddenly started to stutter when speaking. What is the most likely speech problem? The correct answer is C: Evidence of an emotional conflict.
Much of what constitutes stuttering cannot be observed by the listener; this includes such things as sound and word fears, situational fears, anxiety, tension, shame, and a feeling of loss of control during speech. The emotional state of the individual who stutters often constitutes the most difficult aspect of the disorder. If a student suddenly begins to stutter, an investigation into what is happening in the child's life should be initiated.

15. Andy shows up to class abusive and irritable. He is often late, sleeps in class, sometimes slurs his speech, and has an odor of drinking. What is the first intervention to take? The answer is D: Call administration, avoid conflict, and supervise others carefully.
Educators are not only likely to, but often do face students who are high on something. Of course, they are not only a hazard to their own safety and those of others, but their ability to be productive learners is greatly diminished, if not non-existent. They show up instead of skip, because it's not always easy or practical for them to spend the day away from home, but not in school. Unless they can stay inside they are at risk of being picked up for truancy. Some enjoy being high in school, getting a sense of satisfaction by putting something over on the system. Some just don't take drug use seriously enough to think usage at school might be inappropriate. The first responsibility of the teacher is to assure the safety of all of the children. Avoiding conflict with the student who is high and obtaining help from administration is the best course of action.

16. A 16 year-old girl who has been looking sad writes an essay in which the main protagonist commits suicide. You overhear her talking about suicide. What do you do? The answer is C: Report this immediately to school administration. Make your own report to authorities if required by protocol in your school. Do nothing else.
A child who is suicidal is beyond any help that can be offered in a classroom. The first step is to report the situation to administration. If your school protocol calls for it, the situation should also be reported to authorities.

TEACHER STUDY GUIDE

17. You are leading a substance abuse discussion for health class. The students present their belief that marijuana is not harmful to their health. What set of data would refute their claim? The correct answer is B: it damages brain cells, causes behavior changes in prenatally exposed infants, leads to other drug abuse, and causes short-term memory loss.

The student tending toward the use of drugs and /or alcohol will exhibit losses in social and academic functional levels that were previously attained. He may begin to experiment with substances. The adage, "Pot makes a smart kid average and an average kid dumb," is right on the mark. There exist not a few families where pot smoking is a known habit of the parents. The children start their habit by stealing from the parents, making it almost impossible to convince the child that drugs and alcohol are not good for them. Parental use is hampering national efforts to clean up America. The school may be the only source for the real information that children need in order to make intelligent choices about drug use. It's important to remember that if children start using drugs early, it will interfere with their accomplishing developmental tasks and will likely lead to a lifetime of addiction.

18. Jeanne, a bright, attentive student is in first hour English. She is quiet, but very alert, often visually scanning the room in random patterns. Her pupils are dilated and she has a slight but noticeable tremor in her hands. She fails to note a cue given from her teacher. At odd moments she will act as if responding to stimuli that aren't there by suddenly changing her gaze. When spoken to directly, she has a limited response, but her teacher has a sense she is not herself. What should the teacher do? The correct answer is D: Quietly call for administration, remain calm and be careful not to alarm the class.

These behaviors are indicative of drug use. The best thing a teacher can do in this case is call for help from administration.

TEACHER STUDY GUIDE

19. Marcus is a first grade boy of good developmental attainment. His learning progress is good the first half of the year. He shows no indicators of emotional distress. After the holiday break, he returns much changed. He is quieter, sullen even, tending to play alone. He has moments of tearfulness, sometimes almost without cause. He avoids contact with adults as often as he can. Even play with his friends has become limited. He has episodes of wetting not seen before, and often wants to sleep in school. What approach is appropriate for this sudden change in behavior? The correct answer is B: Report this change immediately to administration. Do not call the parents until administration decides a course of action.

Anytime a child's disposition, attitude, or habits change significantly, teachers and parents need to seriously consider the existence of emotional difficulties. Emotional disturbances in childhood are not uncommon and take a variety of forms. Usually these problems show up in the form of uncharacteristic behaviors. Most of the time, children respond favorably to brief treatment programs of psychotherapy. At other times, disturbances may need more intensive therapy and are harder to resolve. All stressful behaviors need to be addressed, and any type of chronic antisocial behavior needs to be examined as a possible symptom of deep-seated emotional upset. In a case where the change is sudden and dramatic, administration needs to become involved.

20. What have recent studies regarding effective teachers concluded? The correct answer is C: Effective teachers state their own policies and establish consistent class rules and procedures on the first day of class.

The teacher can get ahead of the game by stating clearly on the first day of school in her introductory information for the students exactly what the rules. These should be stated firmly but unemotionally. When one of those rules is broken, he/she can then refer to the rules, rendering enforcement much easier to achieve. It's extremely difficult to achieve goals with students who are out of control. Establishing limits early and consistently enforcing them enhances learning. It is also helpful for the teacher to display prominently the classroom rules. This will serve as a visual reminder of the students' expected behaviors. In a study of classroom management procedures, it was established that the combination of conspicuously displayed rules, frequent verbal references to the rules, and appropriate consequences for appropriate behaviors led to increased levels of on-task behavior.

21. To maintain the flow of events in the classroom, what should an effective teacher do? The correct answer is C: Direct attention to content, rather than focusing the class on misbehavior.

Students who misbehave often do so to attract attention. By focusing the attention of the misbehaver as well as the rest of the class on the real purpose of the classroom sends the message that misbehaving will not be rewarded with class attention to the misbehaver. Engaging students in content by using the various tools available to the creative teacher goes a long way in ensuring a peaceful classroom.

OPTE

TEACHER STUDY GUIDE

22. Why is it important for a teacher to pose a question before calling on students to answer? The correct answer is B: It keeps the students as a group focused on the class work.
It doesn't take much distraction for a class's attention to become diffused. Once this happens, effectively teaching a principle or a skill is very difficult. The teacher should plan presentations that will keep students focused on the lesson. A very useful tool is effective, well-thought-out, pointed questions.

23. Which statement is an example of specific praise? C: "Robert, you did a good job staying in line. See how it helped us get to music class on time?"
Praise is a powerful tool in obtaining and maintaining order in a classroom. In addition, it is an effective motivator. It is even more effective if the positive results of good behavior are included.

24. What is one way a teacher can supplement verbal praise? The correct answer is A: Help students evaluate their own performance and supply self-reinforcement.
While praise is useful in maintaining order in a classroom and in motivating students, it's important for the teacher to remember at all times that one major educational objective is that of preparing students to succeed in the world once the supports of the classroom are gone. Self-esteem or lack of it are often barriers to success. An important lesson and skill for students to learn is how to bolster one's own self-esteem and confidence.

25. Reducing off task time and maximizing the amount of time students spend attending to academic tasks is closely related to which of the following? The correct answer is B: Business-like behaviors of the teacher.
The effective teacher continually evaluates his/her own physical/mental/social/emotional well-being with regard to the students in his/her classroom. There is always the tendency to satisfy social and emotional needs through relationships with the students. A good teacher genuinely likes his/her students, and that's a positive thing. However, if students are not convinced that the teacher's purpose for being there is to get a job done, the atmosphere in the classroom becomes difficult to control. This is the job of the teacher. Maintaining a business-like approach in the classroom yields many positive results. It's a little like a benevolent boss.

26. The concept of efficient use of time includes which of the following? The correct answer is D: Punctuality, management transition, and wait time avoidance.
The "benevolent boss" described in the rationale for question 34 applies here. One who succeeds in managing a business follows these rules; so does the successful teacher.

TEACHER STUDY GUIDE

27. What steps are important in the review of subject matter in the classroom? The correct answer is A: A lesson-initiating review, topic, and a lesson-end review.
The effective teacher utilizes all three of these together with comprehension checks to make sure the students are processing the information. Lesson-end reviews are restatements (by the teacher or teacher and students) of the content of discussion at the end of a lesson. Subject matter retention increases when lessons include an outline at the beginning of the lesson and a summary at the end of the lesson. This type of structure is utilized in successful classrooms. Moreover, when students know what is coming next, and what is expected of them, they feel more a part of their learning environment and deviant behavior is lessened.

28. What is a sample of an academic transition signal? The correct answer is D: "That completes the description of cumulus clouds. Now we will look at the description of cirrus clouds."
Transitions are language bridges between one topic and another. The teacher should thoughtfully plan transitions when several topics are going to be presented in one lesson to be sure that students are carried along. Without transitions, sometimes students are still focused on a previous topic and are lost in the discussion.

29. What is an example of a low order question? The correct answer is C: "What items do we recycle in our county"
Remember that the difference between specificity and abstractness is a continuum. The most specific is something that is concrete and can be seen, heard, smelled, tasted, or felt, like cans, bottles, and newspapers. At the other end of the spectrum is an abstraction like importance. Lower-order questions are on the concrete end of the continuum; higher-order questions are on the abstract end.

30. The teacher states that the lesson the students will be engaged in will consist of a review of the material from the previous day, a demonstration of the scientific aspects of an electronic circuit, and small group work on setting up an electronic circuit. What has the teacher demonstrated? The correct answer is B: Giving the general framework for the lesson to facilitate learning.
If children know where they're going, they're more likely to be engaged in getting there. It's important to give them a road map whenever possible for what is coming in their classes.

OPTE

TEACHER STUDY GUIDE

31. Wait-time has what effect? The correct answer is B. Fewer chain and low level questions are asked with more higher level questions included.
One part of the questioning process for the successful teacher is *wait-time*: the time between the question and either the student response or your follow-up. Many teachers vaguely recommend some general amount of wait-time (until the student starts to get uncomfortable or is clearly perplexed), but we focus here on wait-time as a specific and powerful communicative tool that speaks through its structured silences. Embedded in wait-time are subtle clues about your judgments of a student's abilities and your expectations of individuals and groups. For example, the more time you allow a student to mull through a question, the more you trust his or her ability to answer that question without getting flustered. As a rule, the practice of prompting is not a problem. Giving support and helping students reason through difficult conundrums is part of being an effective teacher.

32. What is one benefit of amplifying a student's response? B: It is helpful to other students who are in the process of learning the reasoning or steps in answering the question.
Not only does the teacher show acceptance and give value to student responses by acknowledging, amplifying, discussing or restating the comment or question, she also helps the rest of the class learn to reason. If a student response is allowed, even if it is blurted out, it must be acknowledged and the student made aware of the quality of the response. A teacher acknowledges a student response by commenting on it. For example, the teacher states the definition of a noun, and then asks for examples of nouns in the classroom. A student responds, "My pencil is a noun." The teacher answers, "Okay, let us list that on the board." By this response and the action of writing "pencil" on the board, the teacher has just incorporated the student's response into the lesson. A teacher may also amplify the student response through another question directed to either the original student or to another student. For example, the teacher may say, "Okay," giving the student feedback on the quality of the answer, and then add, "What do you mean by "run" when you say the battery runs the radio?" Another way of showing acceptance and value of student response is to discuss the student response. For example, after a student responds, the teacher would say, "Class, let us think along that line. What is some evidence that proves what Susie just stated?" The teacher may also restate the response. For example, the teacher might say, "So you are saying the seasons are caused by the tilt of the earth. Is this what you said?"

TEACHER STUDY GUIDE

33. A study by Darch and Gersten that examined the effects of positive feedback on the reading performance of seven and eight-year old learning disabled students found which result? The correct answer is B: Students exhibited more on-task behavior.
These two special educators have conducted many studies that are useful in dealing with "exceptional" children. Their findings are influencing the approaches to teaching special education students in many ways, but they are also useful for teachers in regular classrooms who have students who are struggling to keep up. The successful teacher will make use of their findings.

34. When is optimal benefit reached when handling an incorrect student response? The correct answer is C: When the student is redirected to a better problem solving approach.
It's important that students feel confident and comfortable in making responses, knowing that even if they give a wrong answer, they will not be embarrassed. If a student is ridiculed or embarrassed by an incorrect response, the student my shut down and not participate thereafter in classroom discussion. One way to respond to the incorrect answer is to ask the child, "Show me from your book why you think that." This gives the student a chance to correct the answer and redeem himself or herself. Another possible response from the teacher is to use the answer as a non-example. For example, after discussing the characteristics of warm-blooded and cold-blooded animals, the teacher asks for some examples of warm-blooded animals. A student raises his or her hand and responds, "A snake." The teacher could then say, "Remember, snakes lay eggs; they do not have live births. However, a snake is a good non-example of a mammal." The teacher then draws a line down the board and under a heading of "non-example" writes "snake." This action conveys to the child that even though the answer was wrong, it still contributed positively to the class discussion. Notice how the teacher did not digress from the task of listing warm-blooded animals, which in other words is maintaining academic focus, and at the same time allowed the student to maintain dignity.

35. What are the two ways concepts can be taught? B. Inductively and deductively.
Induction is reasoning from the particular to the general—that is, looking at a feature that exists in several examples and drawing a conclusion about that feature. Deduction is the reverse: it's the statement of the generality and then supporting it with specific examples.

36. Using pro-active expressions and repetition has what effect on students? The correct answer is A: Helps student become aware of important elements of content.
Refer to explanation for question 53.

OPTE

37. How can the teacher help students become more work oriented and less disruptive? The correct answer is B: Challenge the students with a task and show genuine enthusiasm for it.
Many studies have demonstrated that the enthusiasm of the teacher is infectious. If students feel that the teacher is ambivalent about a task, they will also catch that attitude.

38. What is an effective way to prepare students for testing? The correct answer is B: Orient the students to the test, telling them of the purpose, how the results will be used and how it is relevant to them.
If a test is to be an accurate measure of achievement, it must test the information, not the format of the test itself. If students know ahead of time what the test will be like, why they are taking it, what the teacher will do with the results, and what it has to do with them, the exercise is more likely to result in a true measure of what they've learned.

39. How will students have a fair chance to demonstrate what they know on a test? The correct answer is B: The examiner provides a comfortable setting free of distractions and positively encourages the students.
Taking a test is intimidating to students at best. In addition, some students are unable to focus when there are distractions. Feeling that the teacher is on their side helps students relax and truly demonstrate what they have learned on a test.

40. What is an example of formative feedback? The correct answer is C: Verbal behavior that expresses approval of a student response to a test item.
Standardized testing is currently under great scrutiny but educators agree that any test that serves as a means of gathering and interpreting information about children's learning and which can provide accurate, helpful input for nurturing children's further growth, is acceptable. All testing must be formative in nature. Formative evaluation is the basic, everyday kind of assessment that teachers continually do to understand students' growth and to help them learn further.

41. How could a KWL chart be used in instruction? The correct answer is B: To assess prior knowledge of the students.
To understand information, not simply repeat it, students must connect it to their previous understanding. Textbooks can't do that. Instead, teachers—the people who know students best—have to find out what they know and how to build on that knowledge. In science, having students make predictions before conducting experiments is an obvious way of finding out what they know, and having them compare their observations to those predictions helps connect new knowledge and old. In history, teachers can also ask students what they know about a topic before they begin studying it or ask them to make predictions about what they will learn. KWL charts, in which students discuss what they know, what they want to know, and (later) what they have learned, are one way to activate this prior knowledge.

42. How can the teacher establish a positive climate in the classroom? The correct answer is A: Help students see the unique contributions of individual differences.
In the first place, an important purpose of education is to prepare students to live successfully in the real world, and this is an important insight and understanding for them to take into that world. In the second place, the most fertile learning environment is one in which all viewpoints and backgrounds are respected and where everyone has equal respect.

43. How can students use a computer desktop publishing center? The correct answer is B: To create student made books.
By creating a book, students gain new insights into how communication works. Suddenly, the concept of audience for what they write and create becomes real. They also have an opportunity to be introduced to graphic arts, an exploding field. In addition, just as computers are a vital part of the world they will be entering as adults, so is desktop publishing. It is universally used by businesses of all kinds.

44. Which of the following is an example of a synthesis question according to Bloom's taxonomy? The correct answer is D: "Propose an alternative to_____."
There are six levels to the taxonomy: Knowledge, Comprehension, Application, Analysis, Synthesis, and Evaluation. Synthesis is compiling information together in a different way by combining elements in a new pattern or proposing alternative solutions to produce a unique communication, plan, or proposed set of operations or to derive a set of abstract relations.

45. What is a good strategy for teaching ethnically diverse students? The correct answer is D: Include ethnic studies in the curriculum.
Exploring a students' own cultures increases their confidence levels in the group. It is also a very useful tool when students are struggling to develop identities that they can feel comfortable with. The bonus is that this is good training for living in the world.

46. How many stages of intellectual development does Piaget define? The correct answer is B: Four.
The stages are:
1. Sensorimotor stage: from birth to age 2 years (children experience the world through movement and senses).
2. Preoperational stage: from ages 2 to 7(acquisition of motor skills).
3. Concrete operational stage: from ages 7 to 11 (children begin to think logically about concrete events).
4. Formal Operational stage: after age 11 (development of abstract reasoning).

TEACHER STUDY GUIDE

47. What is the most significant development emerging in children at age two? The correct answer is C: Language develops.
Language begins to develop in an infant not long after birth. Chomsky claims that children teach themselves to speak using the people around them for resources. Several studies of the sounds infants make in their cribs seems to support this. The first stage of meaningful sounds is the uttering of a word that obviously has meaning for the child, for example, "bird" when the child sees one flying through the air. Does the development of real language begin when the noun is linked with a verb ("bird fly")? When language begins and how it develops has been debated for a long time. It's useful for a teacher to investigate those theories and studies.

48. According to Piaget, when does the development of symbolic functioning and language take place? The correct answer is D: Preoperational stage.
Although there is no general theory of cognitive development, the most historically influential theory was developed by Jean Piaget, a Swiss psychologist (1896-1980). His theory provided many central concepts in the field of developmental psychology. His theory concerned the growth of intelligence, which for Piaget meant the ability to more accurately represent the world and perform logical operations on representations of concepts grounded in the world. His theory concerns the emergence and acquisition of schemata—schemes of how one perceives the world—in "developmental stages," times when children are acquiring new ways of mentally representing information. His theory is considered "constructivist," meaning that, unlike nativist theories (which describe cognitive development as the unfolding of innate knowledge and abilities) or empiricist theories (which describe cognitive development as the gradual acquisition of knowledge through experience), asserts that we construct our cognitive abilities through self-motivated action in the world. For his development of the theory, Piaget was awarded the Erasmus Prize.

49. What is the learning theorist's view of language acquisition? The correct answer is A: Language is shaped by the reinforcement children receive from their caretakers.
Chomsky, for instance, conducted studies on children that revealed that they actually teach themselves their own language by using the adults around them for reference. When a baby is playing with various sounds and happens to say "mama," the family goes bananas, so the baby keeps that sound! And so forth. Parents and others, of course, take their roles as language purveyors seriously, pointing out a bird and repeating it for the child until the child begins to echo a facsimile of that sound, which is *rewarded* by the adult doing the "teaching." Once children are in school, many of the same principles are in place. If the teacher rewards a usage, either printed or spoken, the child will be more likely to forge ahead and add more opportunities for reward.

OPTE

TEACHER STUDY GUIDE

50. Bobby, a nine year-old, has been caught stealing frequently in the classroom. What might be a factor contributing to this behavior? The correct answer is B: Serious emotional disturbance.

Lying, stealing, and fighting are atypical behaviors that most children may exhibit occasionally, but if a child lies, steals, or fights regularly or blatantly, then these behaviors may be indicative of emotional distress. Emotional disturbances in childhood are not uncommon and take a variety of forms. Usually these problems show up in the form of uncharacteristic behaviors. Most of the time, children respond favorably to brief treatment programs of psychotherapy. At other times, disturbances may need more intensive therapy and are harder to resolve. All stressful behaviors need to be addressed, and any type of chronic antisocial behavior needs to be examined as a possible symptom of deep-seated emotional upset.

51. What does the validity of a test refer to? The correct answer is B: Its usefulness.

the *Joint technical standards for educational and psychological testing* (APA, AERA, NCME, 1985) states: "Validity is the most important consideration in test evaluation. The concept refers to the appropriateness, meaningfulness and usefulness of *the specific inferences made from test scores*. Test validation is the process of accumulating evidence to support such inferences. A variety of inferences may be made from scores produced by a given test, and there are many ways of accumulating evidence to support any particular inference. Validity, however, is a unitary concept. Although evidence may be accumulated in many ways, validity always refers to the degree to which that evidence supports the inferences that are made from test scores."

52. What is the best definition for an achievement test? The correct answer is B: It measures broad areas of knowledge that are the result of cumulative learning experiences.

The ways that a teacher uses test data is a meaningful aspect of instruction and may increase the motivation level of the students especially when this information is available in the form of feedback to the students. This feedback should indicate to the students what they need to do in order to improve their achievement. Frequent testing and feedback is most often an effective way to increase achievement.

OPTE

TEACHER STUDY GUIDE

53. Which of the following is an accurate description of ESL students? C: Are not a homogeneous group.

Because ESL students are often grouped in classes that take a different approach to teaching English than those for native speakers, it's easy to assume that they all present with the same needs and characteristics. Nothing could be further from the truth, even in what they need when it comes to learning English. It's important that their backgrounds and personalities be observed just as with native speakers. It was very surprising several years ago when Vietnamese children began arriving in American schools with little training in English and went on to excel in their classes, often even beyond their American counterparts. In many schools, there were Vietnamese merit scholars in the graduating classes.

54. What is an effective way to help a non-English speaking student succeed in class? The correct answer is B: Maintain an encouraging, success-oriented atmosphere.

Anyone who is in an environment where his language is not the standard one feels embarrassed and inferior. The student who is in that situation expects to fail. Encouragement is even more important for these students. They need many opportunities to succeed.

55. What should be considered when evaluating textbooks for content? The correct answer is C: Free of cultural stereotyping.

While textbook writers and publishers have responded to the need to be culturally diverse in recent years, a few texts are still being offered that don't meet these standards. When teachers have an opportunity to be involved in choosing textbooks, they can be watchdogs for the community in keeping the curriculum free of matter that reinforces bigotry and discrimination.

56. How can texts be modified for low-level ESL students? The correct answer is A: Add visuals and illustrations.

No matter what name we put on it, a book is a book. If students can see the object, not only will they be able to compare their own word for it, a useful tool in learning a new language, but the object can serve as a mnemonic device. The teacher might use actual objects in a classroom to facilitate learning the new language.

57. Which of the following is considered a study skill? The correct answer is A: Using graphs, tables, and maps.

In studying, it is certainly true that "a picture is worth a thousand words." Not only are these devices useful in making a point clear, they are excellent mnemonic devices for remembering facts.

TEACHER STUDY GUIDE

58. When using a kinesthetic approach, what would be an appropriate activity? The correct answer is :. Match.
Brain lateralization theory emerged in the 1970s and demonstrated that the left hemisphere appeared to be associated with verbal and sequential abilities whereas the right hemisphere appeared to be associated with emotions and with spatial, holistic processing. Although those particular conclusions continue to be challenged, it is clear that people concentrate, process, and remember new and difficult information under very different conditions. For example, auditory and visual perceptual strengths, passivity, and self-oriented or authority-oriented motivation often correlate with high academic achievement, whereas tactual and kinesthetic strengths, a need for mobility, nonconformity, and peer motivation often correlate with school underachievement (Dunn & Dunn, 1992, 1993). Understanding how students perceive the task of learning new information differently is often helpful in tailoring the classroom experience for optimal success.

59. Etienne is an ESL student. He has begun to engage in conversation which produces a connected narrative. What developmental stage for second language acquisition is he in? D: Intermediate fluency.
Attaining total fluency usually takes several years although the younger the learner, the shorter the time it takes.

60. What is a roadblock to second language learning? The correct answer is A: Students are forced to speak.
It's embarrassing for anyone who is in a foreign-language environment to be forced to expose his inability to use that language before he is ready. Being flexible with these students until they're ready to try their wings will shorten the time it will take to approach fluency.

61. What do cooperative learning methods all have in common? B: Cooperative task/cooperative reward structures.
Cooperative learning situations, as practiced in today's classrooms, grew out of searches conducted by several groups in the early 1970's. Cooperative learning situations can range from very formal applications such as STAD (Student Teams-Achievement Divisions) and CIRC (Cooperative Integrated Reading and Composition) to less formal groupings known variously as "group investigation," "learning together," and "discovery groups." Cooperative learning as a general term is now firmly recognized and established as a teaching and learning technique in American schools. Since cooperative learning techniques are so widely diffused in the schools, it is necessary to orient students in the skills by which cooperative learning groups can operate smoothly, and thereby enhance learning. Students who cannot interact constructively with other students will not be able to take advantage of the learning opportunities provided by the cooperative learning situations and will furthermore deprive their fellow students of the opportunity for cooperative learning.

TEACHER STUDY GUIDE

62. Who developed the theory of multiple intelligences? The correct answer is B: Gardner.
Howard Gardner's most famous work is probably *Frames of Mind*, which details seven dimensions of intelligence (Visual/Spatial Intelligence, Musical Intelligence, Verbal Intelligence, Logical/Mathematical Intelligence, Interpersonal Intelligence, Intrapersonal Intelligence, and Bodily/Kinesthetic Intelligence). Gardner's claim that pencil and paper IQ tests do not capture the full range of human intelligences has garnered much praise within the field of education but has also met criticism, largely from psychometricians. Since the publication of *Frames of Mind*, Gardner has additionally identified the 8th dimension of intelligence: Naturalist Intelligence, and is still considering a possible ninth—Existentialist Intelligence.

63. According to research, what can be a result of specific teacher actions on behavior? The correct answer is A: Increase in student misconduct.
Unfortunately, at times misbehavior is the result of specific teacher actions. There is considerable research that indicates that some teacher behavior is upsetting to students and increases the occurrence of student misbehavior. Such teacher behavior may include any action that a child perceives as being unfair, punitive remarks about the child, his behavior or his work, or harsh responses to the child.
Teachers also need to be aware that much of what they say and do can be motivating and may have a positive effect on students' achievement. Studies have been conducted to determine the impact of teacher behavior on student performance. Surprisingly, a teacher's voice can really make an impression on students. Teachers' voices have several dimensions—volume, pitch, rate, etc. A recent study on the effects of speech rate indicates that, although both boys and girls prefer to listen at the rate of about 200 words per minute, boys tend to prefer slower rates overall than girls. This same study indicates that a slower rate of speech directly affects processing ability and comprehension. Other speech factors such as communication of ideas, communication of emotion, distinctness/pronunciation, quality variation and phrasing, correlate with teaching criterion scores. These scores show that "good" teachers ("good" meaning teachers who positively impact and motivate students) use more variety in speech than do "less effective" teachers. A teacher's speech skills can be strong motivating elements. A teacher's body language has an even greater effect on student achievement and ability to set and focus on goals. Teacher smiles provide support and give feedback about the teacher's affective state. A deadpan expression can actually be a detriment to the student's progress. Teacher frowns are perceived by students to mean displeasure, disapproval, and even anger. Studies also show that teacher posture and movement are indicators of the teacher's enthusiasm and energy, which emphatically influence student learning, attitudes, motivation, and focus on goals. Teachers have a greater efficacy on student motivation than any person other than parents.

TEACHER STUDY GUIDE

64. What is the definition of proactive classroom management? The correct answer is C: Management that gives clear and explicit instructions and rewards compliance.
Classroom management plans should be in place when the school year begins. Developing a management plan takes a proactive approach—that is, decide what behaviors will be expected of the class as a whole, anticipate possible problems, and teach the behaviors early in the school year. Involving the students in the development of the classroom rules lets the students know the rationale for the rules, allows them to assume responsibility in the rules because they had a part in developing them.

65. What might be a result if the teacher is distracted by some unrelated event in the instruction? The correct answer is D: Students will lose the momentum of the lesson.
The teacher who can attend to a task situation and an extraneous situation simultaneously without becoming immersed in either one is said to have "with-it-ness." This ability is absolutely imperative for teacher effectiveness and success. It can be a difficult task to address deviant behavior while sustaining academic flow, but this is a skill that teachers need to develop early in their careers and one that will become second nature, intuitive, instinctive. Teacher with-it-ness is defined as "teacher behavior that indicates to the students that the teacher knows what she is doing" at all times and at the same time can continue instruction. With-it-ness has been found to positively affect both classroom behavior management and student task involvement. Teachers who have been specially trained in with-it-ness, report positive correlation between their with-it-ness and reading achievement as well as reductions in student misbehaviors and disruptions.

66. Why is praise for compliance important in classroom management? The correct answer is B: Desirable conduct will be repeated.
The tried-and-true principle that behavior that is rewarded will be repeated is demonstrated here. If other students laugh at a child's misbehavior, he will repeat it. On the other hand, if the teach rewards the behaviors she wants to see repeated, it is likely to happen.

OPTE

TEACHER STUDY GUIDE

67. What is an effective amount of "wait time"? The correct answer is B: 5 seconds.

In formal training, most preservice teachers are taught the art of questioning. One part of the questioning process is *wait-time*: the time between the question and either the student response or your follow-up. Many teachers vaguely recommend some general amount of wait-time (until the student starts to get uncomfortable or is clearly perplexed), but we focus here on wait-time as a specific and powerful communicative tool that speaks through its structured silences. Embedded in wait-time are subtle clues about your judgments of a student's abilities and your expectations of individuals and groups. For example, the more time you allow a student to mull through a question, the more you trust his or her ability to answer that question without getting flustered.

As a rule, the practice of prompting is not a problem. Giving support and helping students reason through difficult conundrums is part of being an effective teacher.

68. Mr. Perez has the pictures and maps ready for his lesson. The movie is set up to go, and he tested the operation of the machine before the class came in. What is this an example of? The correct answer is B: Housekeeping.

Housekeeping is when a "teacher routinizes activities such as passing papers out, moving to get books, writing on the board, etc., and has materials prepared, procedures worked out, and everything in order." Additionally, effective teachers have highly planned lessons with all materials in order prior to class. This is referred to as management of instructional material and defines it as "teacher preparation of materials that are to be used for a particular segment of instruction readily available." In other words, if a teacher is going to utilize a chart or a map in a lesson, the chart or map is already prepared and in place in the classroom before class begins. Furthermore, all materials are copied and in order ready to pass out as needed. This results in the efficient distribution of materials and leads to less off-task time. Therefore, effective teachers routinize daily housekeeping activities to minimize the amount of time spent on them. Additionally, they have all materials prepared prior to class and in order to facilitate speedy distribution.

69. How are standardized tests useful in assessment? The correct answer is D: For comparison to the population on which the test was normed.

While the efficacy of the standardized tests that are being used nationally has come under attack recently, they are, actually the only device for comparing where an individual student stands with a wide range of peers. They also provide a measure for a program or a school to evaluate how their own students are doing as compared to the populace at large. Even so, they should not be the only measure upon which decisions are made or evaluations drawn. There are many other instruments for measuring student achievement that the teacher needs to consult and take into account.

OPTE

70. Ms. Smith says, "Yes, exactly what do you mean by 'It was the author's intention to mislead you.'" What does this illustrate? The correct answer is C: Probes a response.
From ancient times notable teachers such as Socrates and Jesus have employed oral-questioning to enhance their discourse, to stimulate thinking, and/or to stir emotion among their audiences. Educational researchers and practitioners virtually all agree that teachers' effective use of questioning promotes student learning . Effective teachers continually develop their questioning skills.

71. What is perhaps the most controversial issue in developmental psychology? The correct answer is B. Nature vs. nurture.
Nature versus nurture is a shorthand expression for debates about the relative importance of an individual's innate qualities ("nature") versus personal experiences ("nurture") in determining or causing individual differences in physical and behavioral traits. The phrase nature vs. nurture was first used by Francis Galton, possibly in reference to Shakespeare's Caliban—*A devil, a born devil, on whose nature Nurture can never stick* (from *The Tempest*). The controversy has heated up since the genetic code has been broken and it has become common knowledge that each person's DNA makes him or her unique.

72. A child exhibits the following symptoms: a lack of emotional responsivity, indifference to physical contact, abnormal social play, and abnormal speech. What is the likely diagnosis for this child? The correct answer is C: Autism.
According to many psychologists who have been involved with treating autistic children, it seems that these children have built a wall between themselves and everyone else, including their families and even their parents. They do not make eye contact with others and do not even appear to hear the voices of those who speak to them. They cannot empathize with others and have no ability to appreciate humor. The prognosis for autistic children is painfully discouraging. Only about five percent of autistic children become socially well adjusted in adulthood. Another twenty percent make fair social adjustments. The remaining seventy-five percent are socially incapacitated and must be supervised for the duration of their lives. Treatment may include outpatient psychotherapy, drugs, or long-term treatment in a residential center, but neither the form of treatment nor even the lack of treatment seems to make a difference in the long run.

73. What is not a way that teachers show acceptance and give value to a student response? The correct answer is B. Correcting.
There are ways to treat every answer as worthwhile even if it happens to be wrong. The objective is to keep students involved in the dialogue. If their efforts to participate are "rewarded" with what seems to them to be a rebuke or that leads to embarrassment, they will be less willing to respond the next time.

TEACHER STUDY GUIDE

74. What is teacher withitness? The correct answer is D: Attending to two tasks at once.

The teacher who knows his/her class well and is "with-it" will be cognizant of what is happening in every corner of the classroom between and among the children at all times. It should be relatively easy to identify problems that occur during the school day since the teacher observes the students as they interact with one another. Should the teacher be unaware of problems between students, misbehavior will surely occur. At this point in time the teacher will then tune in to the child who is misbehaving and hopefully, will soon be able to see what is happening to cause misbehaviors. As with anything else, the best way to solve behavior problems is to prevent them. The "with-it" teacher frequently knows when and why problems will occur and will act to eliminate potential provocation. The simplest means of preventing conflict between students who are having a problem with one another is to give them their own space and to separate them.

Teacher with-it-ness is defined as "teacher behavior that indicates to the students that the teacher knows what they are doing" at all times and at the same time can continue instruction. With-it-ness has been found to positively affect both classroom behavior management and student task involvement. Teachers who have been specially trained in with-it-ness, report positive correlation between their with-it-ness and reading achievement as well as reductions in student misbehaviors and disruptions. Teacher training in with-it-ness techniques includes:

a) implementing positive questioning techniques
b) using alerting cues
c) giving goal-directed prompts
d) using a soft voice when making reprimands
e) integrating alternative behavior desists
f) applying concurrent and specific praise

Research in regard to teacher with-it-ness indicate that teachers who are comfortable with the above techniques and are "with-it" increase instructional time by at least twenty minutes per day and decrease deviant behavior significantly. Further, with-it-ness techniques have been found to apply to boys as well as girls, to emotionally disturbed children as well as non-disturbed children, and to both younger and older grade children. They also apply to the entire class as well as to individual students.

OPTE

75. What should the teacher do when a student is tapping a pencil on the desk during a lecture? The correct answer is B: Walk over to the student and quietly touch the pencil as a signal for the student to stop.

An assertive discipline plan should be developed as soon as the teacher meets the students. The students can become involved in developing and discussing the needs for the rules. Rules should be limited to four to six basic classroom rules that are simple to remember and positively stated (For example, raise hand to speak, instead of, don't talk without permission).

1. Recognize and remove roadblocks to assertive discipline. Replace negative expectations with positives, and set reasonable limits for the children.
2. Practice an assertive response style. That is, clearly state teacher expectations and expect the students to comply with them.
3. Set limits. Take into consideration the students' behavioral needs, the teacher's expectations, and set limits for behavior. Decide what you will do when the rules are broken or complied with.
4. Follow through promptly with the consequences when students break the rules. However, the students should clearly know in advance what to expect when a rule is broken. Conversely, also follow through with the promised rewards for compliance and good behavior. This reinforces the concept that individuals choose their behavior and that there are consequences for their behavior.
5. Devise a system of positive consequences. Positive consequences do not have to always be food or treats. However, rewards should not be promised if it is not possible to deliver them. The result is a more positive classroom.

TEACHER STUDY GUIDE

SAMPLE CONSTRUCTED-RESPONSE MODULES

The content covered by the modules described below is assessed through the constructed-response component of the Oklahoma Professional Teaching Examination. The test consists of three constructed response modules, and examples are provided below.

CRITICAL ANALYSIS MODULE: Learners and the Learning Environment

This module requires candidates to construct written responses that demonstrate an understanding of aspects of professional knowledge as described in Subarea I. Assignments and responses for this module will relate to Competencies 0001, 0002, 0003, and/or 0004 of the test framework.

This component of the assessment requires candidates to exercise critical thinking skills to analyze educational issues related to learners and the learning environment and present their own opinions in a coherent and convincing way.

For example, the candidate is presented with a brief summary of a contemporary educational issue or topic (e.g., student development patterns, theories of learning, motivational techniques). The candidate responds in writing by presenting his or her own point of view on the topic and supporting that position with reasoned arguments and appropriate examples.

SAMPLE ASSIGNMENT:

You will now be asked to analyze and discuss an educational issue related to Subarea 1 of the OPTE test framework, "Learners and the Learning Environment"

Respond to the following Critical Analysis Module Assignment:

> Student Learning: Standards-Driven or Project-Based?

In an age of accountability for student learning, many educators assume that sticking to standards and ensuring that each standard is covered explicitly is the safest and most prudent thing to do. However, there are still many educators that believe that standards can be covered, perhaps in a non-linear fashion, by engaging students in academic and cross-curricular projects. Those who believe that project-based instruction is more valuable suggest that students will enjoy their learning more and will still learn many important academic standards in the process.

TEACHER STUDY GUIDE

Those who believe that standards-driven learning is more valuable might argue that it is unfair to students to not cover each and every area that they will be tested on. They might also suggest that teaching standards in a linear fashion will provide greater clarity for students.

In a response written for an audience of teachers, use your knowledge of learners and the learning environment to analyze and discuss the issue of standards-driven and project-based teaching.

RESPONSE:

There is no doubt that students must be prepared based on state standards. However, when analyzing state standards, it is important to realize that while standards may look like a bunch of unconnected skills, they really do build upon one another and there is quite a bit of information that overlaps. In my first year as a high school Language Arts teacher, I know that it is important to focus both on standards as well as engaging, meaningful projects. I do not believe that a teacher would have to choose between the two approaches, standards-driven and project-based.

When evaluating what to teach and how to teach it, it is important first to ensure that what is being taught can be defended by the standards. Teachers must make sure that students learn what is required, as students are tested on that material. They are also expected to know that material as they progress to the next grade level.

However, not all students will learn at the same pace and in the same way. Furthermore, if a teacher were to simply "cover" the standards, students would have little context for understanding the material, and it certainly would not be very exciting. Students need to feel that what they are learning is important beyond passing tests. For that reason, developing lessons, units, and projects that take students' varied learning styles into account and draw upon real-world examples and issues will make learning more fun, and it will ensure that all students learn. However, such lessons, units, and projects should also be based on standards so that students have interesting, enjoyable, and student-centered ways of learning the information they are required to know. This method seems to be a more logical approach that combines the positives of both positions.

OPTE

An example of combining these two approaches, based on a secondary Language Arts classroom, is the teaching of literature. For example, a particular standard might call for students to understand imagery in literature. Another standard might call for students to learn about specific eras in American literature. Another might call for students to learn how to write an analysis of literary techniques. If I were to teach based on standards-driven principles, I would teach all these skills out of context. Yet, if I were to focus simply on a project-based method, I might not hit any of these issues. However, if I were to have students engage in a project that focused on each of these areas and gave them choice in the way they work toward the final project, while giving specialized assistance to those who need it, students will get the opportunity to learn these skills, and they will more likely enjoy the process and learn at an appropriate pace.

Combining both approaches seems most logical. While many educators argue that standards-drive instruction is the only way to ensure that students are prepared for testing, doing so alone will provide little opportunity for students to learn in ways that are natural for them. On the other hand, while many educators are convinced that doing anything other than project-based instruction will be boring for students, not paying significant attention to standards will ensure that students are not prepared for the complex academic tasks they will be required to master.

EVALUATION:

The assignment asked the candidate to analyze two claims, both at odds with each other. One side, suggesting that standards-driven instruction is more appropriate, seemingly goes against the other side, project-based instruction. Yet the candidate wrote an essay that effectively found the best of both methods. The essay demonstrates a deep knowledge of student learning, as well as contemporary issues of curriculum and instruction. It demonstrated knowledge of student engagement and standards-based instruction. Although the essay did not ask for the candidate to demonstrate the best of both models, its strength lies in the fact that it does indeed show how both methods have some limitations as well as some strengths. Putting both together with a good curricular example was effective. This essay demonstrates strong knowledge of Subarea 1 of the OPTE framework.

TEACHER STUDY GUIDE

STUDENT INQUIRY MODULE: Instruction and Assessment

This module requires candidates to construct written responses that demonstrate an understanding of aspects of professional knowledge as described in Subarea II. Assignments and responses for this module will relate to Competencies 0005, 0006, 0007, 0008, and/or 0009 of the test framework.

This component of the assessment requires the candidate to apply general principles of teaching and learning in planning, delivering, and adapting instruction and assessment. For example, the candidate is presented with an instructional goal (e.g., fostering students' critical thinking skills, providing opportunities for students to explore a topic using a range of learning modes, helping students relate instructional content to their own experience). The candidate responds in writing by describing and evaluating instructional strategies and activities designed to help students attain that goal.

SAMPLE ASSIGNMENT:

You will now be asked to demonstrate your knowledge of Subarea II, Instruction and Assessment.

Respond to the following Student Inquiry Module assignment:

LEARNING GOAL: Students will learn and apply new information through the use of hands-on activities.

In a written response for an audience of teachers, identify a grade/age level and subject area for which you are prepared to teach, then use your knowledge of instruction and assessment to:

- Describe a "hands-on" activity or lesson that would help students to learn and apply new information.
- Explain why this "hands-on" activity or lesson would be helpful in teaching students new information.

RESPONSE:

    For a second grade math lesson, I might end up teaching students about fractions. While fractions are difficult to learn about with just numbers, using manipulatives and hands-on activities, students will quickly understand the concept of fractions much faster. I would begin a series of lessons on fractions with a hands-on activity that would start with me modeling the activity. Then, students would work in groups to practice on their own.

The first step of this lesson would involve me at the overhead projector. I would draw a picture of a pie on the overhead and suggest that I was going to have five friends over to help me eat it. I would ask students, "So, how am I going to make sure everyone has the same amount of pie?" I would then start to draw lines all over the place—one piece would be very large, a few pieces would be quite small, and the last few would be regular pieces of pie. I would ask students if this looked right. Hopefully, they will say that the pieces are a variety of different sizes. I would then ask them to help me cut the pie so that everyone would have a similar-sized slice. I would end the activity by asking them how many slices I had of ONE pie. They should be able to say that we have six slices.

The next step would be to get the students into groups of three to four students. I would give them cut-outs of a variety of different items. The first would be a pizza. I would then ask them to determine how many slices they would need in order to make sure everyone got one similarly-sized slice. They would have to cut the pizza so that everyone gets the same sized slice. With another paper pizza, they would have to include leftovers for two friends. With yet another paper pizza, they would have to include leftover for each of them for the next day. After cutting out various-sized slices on each pizza, I would have them count up how many slices they got from each pizza.

The final step of this "hands-on" lesson would be to have them, in groups, show me what one-half a pizza would be. On each pizza, they would count up how many slices they have. This would go on and on until they understand that one-half or one-quarter could constitute a variety of numbers of slices depending how many slices were cut for each pizza.

This activity would help students learn the concept of fractions by giving them a practical, simple method of seeing fractions. They would understand that one pizza could have many different combinations of slices. Because they are the same sized pizzas, each one-half or one-quarter would constitute the same size, yet have different numbers of slices. They would be able to learn the concept by applying it with a simple hands-on activity that involves dividing something for friends and leftovers, something they are already familiar with. Overall, this is a fun, practical, and useful way to teach the very difficult concept of fractions.

EVALUATION:

This essay demonstrates a very good knowledge of "hands-on" activities in the teaching of math. It clearly shows how various concepts of instruction can be tailored for different learning styles and different instructional standards. The candidate shows a good working knowledge of the Subarea by demonstrating the importance of carefully designing a lesson in order to meet students' learning needs. The lesson is very clear, and directions are provided step-by-step. No element of instruction is left out. Furthermore, the essay ends with a very good overview of how this lesson would meet students' learning needs, and it argues convincingly for using hands-on methods to teach this concept. Finally, the candidate chose a topic for which hands-on instruction would be very appropriate.

TEACHER STUDY GUIDE

TEACHER ASSIGNMENT MODULE: The Professional Environment

This module requires candidates to construct written responses that demonstrate an understanding of aspects of professional knowledge as described in Subarea III. Assignments and responses for this module will relate to Competencies 0010, 0011, 0012, and/or 0013 of the test framework.

This component of the assessment requires the candidate to reflect on and apply knowledge of the professional roles and responsibilities of the teacher. For example, the candidate is presented with a situation arising from an interaction with colleagues, parents/guardians, or community members and requiring some form of action. The candidate responds in writing by identifying and discussing important issues raised by the situation, describing an appropriate course of action, and explaining how the proposed action is likely to lead to a desirable outcome.

SAMPLE ASSIGNMENT:

In the following Teacher Assignment Module, you will be asked to use your knowledge of Subarea III of the OPTE test framework, "The Professional Environment."

Respond to the following Teacher Assignment Module assignment:

Half-way through the school year, a week after semester report cards are sent home, you get an email from a student's parent complaining that you gave her son low grades for no good reason. She suggests that she has heard nothing but complaints about your teaching and that if you were a better teacher, her son would not have such low grades. She wants to (a) meet with you and the principal together, (b) examine other students' grades to see how her son's grades compare, and (c) have you put together extra credit work so that her son can raise her grade.

In a written response to an audience of educators, use your knowledge of the professional environment to:

- Identify the important issues at stake in this scenario.
- Describe a plan of action you would take to remedy this problem.
- Explain why your plan would be effective in resolving the issue.

OPTE

TEACHER STUDY GUIDE

RESPONSE:

The primary concern in this scenario is the difference of opinion about the student's academic standing in the class. Obviously, the teacher felt that the student deserved a particular grade, and the parent believes that the grade should be higher. This is an issue of assessment, but it is also an issue of politics, parent-school relations, and legalities.

As a teacher, I would do whatever I could to be fair to all students, including the student under question. I would not immediately change the grade, nor would I ignore the parent's concern. In general, I would want to begin by collecting data on the issue, inform the principal, and appropriately interact with the parent. I would not, however, allow the parent to view other students' grades, as this would be illegal.

First, I would inform the principal that a concern has come up regarding a student's grade. I would let the principal know my plan for dealing with this, and I would suggest that a meeting may be necessary. Even though I would have to come back to the principal to discuss the issue in further detail later, I would simply want the principal to know that an incident has occurred so that he/she would be informed and so that I could document that I have gone through all the proper chains of command.

Second, I would do some investigation on my own grading practices, as well as the student's work. Because I would have documented progress and all grades carefully, as well as compiled portfolios of all my students' work, I would not have any problem in accessing the information I would need to determine if I had made an error in evaluation. While reviewing this information, I would document everything I find.

Third, I would collect all scoring guides, rubrics, assignments, and other materials that would explain *how* I evaluated students. I would make sure that I could see a clear documentation in my grading based on the criteria students were aware of when they completed the work.

Fourth, I would convene a meeting with the student's parent and the principal. Although I would bring my documentation, I would want to start by listening to the parent's concerns over her perceptions of my teaching. I would take those concerns seriously and write each one down to demonstrate respect. No matter what, I would review with the parent all the material I brought. However, I would want to end the meeting by offering a "win-win" solution. I would encourage the parent to work with me to determine how her son could get good grades for the next semester.

Of course, if I found an error in my evaluation, I would ensure that the grade be changed. However, under no circumstances would it be fair to offer extra credit to one student and not the others.

What this scenario tells me is that I would want to keep in constant contact with parents, particularly of students whose grades were low throughout the semester. While I would have to back-track in this scenario, I would ensure that in future semesters, I never let a student get to a low grade without first having conferences with the student and his/her parent. This scenario also suggests that evaluation is not just about grades. It's about ensuring that students have been properly prepared for what they will be assessed on. It's also about making sure that assessment is fair and utilized for the purpose of tracking students' progress. If, for example, some students' progress shows little growth, that would be a sign to me to deal with those issues immediately.

As a summary, my method of dealing with this scenario shows respect in the student and parent, yet it relies on careful methods of evaluation of student progress. It demonstrates that it is important to be courteous to parents and to keep principals informed of incidents. Documentation is also crucial in many ways so that students and parents can be assured that fairness will be applied in all aspects of a teacher's class.

EVALUATION:

This response offers a very detailed and comprehensive explanation of a strategy that could be followed for any disagreement about grades. What is most promising about this response is that it goes beyond the incident itself to show how respect, documentation, and full disclosure are important in the field of teaching. In many ways, it also demonstrates a careful process of applying fairness to the classroom.

TEACHER STUDY GUIDE

STATE MAJOR COMPONENTS RETAINED AND CHANGES OF IDEA 2004

The second revision of IDEA occurred in 2004, IDEA was re-authorized as the Individuals with Disabilities Education Improvement Act of 2004 (IDEIA 2004) is commonly referred to as IDEA 2004. IDEA 2004 was effective July 1, 2005.

It was the intention to improve IDEA by adding the philosophy and understanding that special education students need preparation for further study beyond the high school setting by teaching compensatory methods. Accordingly, IDEA 2004 provided a close tie to PL 89-10, the Elementary and Special Education Act of 1965, and stated that students with special needs should have maximum access to the general curriculum. This was defined as the amount for an individual student to reach his fullest potential. Full inclusion was stated not to be the only option by which to achieve this, and specified that skills should be taught to compensate students later in life in cases where inclusion was not the best setting.

IDEA 2004 added a new requirement for special education teachers on the secondary level enforcing NCLBs "Highly Qualified" requirements in the subject area of their curriculum. The rewording in this part of IDEA states that they shall be "no less qualified" than teachers in the core areas.

Free and Appropriate Public Education (FAPE), was revised by mandating that students have maximum access to appropriate general education. Additionally, LRE placement for those students with disabilities must have the same school placement rights as those students who are not disabled. IDEA 2004 recognizes that due to the nature of some disabilities, appropriate education may vary in the amount of participation / placement in the general education setting. For some students, FAPE will mean a choice as to the type of educational institution they attend (private school for example), any of which must provide the special education services deemed necessary for the student through the IEP.

The definition of *Assistive technology devices* was amended to exclude devices that are surgically implanted (i.e. cochlear implants), and clarified that students with assistive technology devices shall not be prevented from having special education services. Assistive technology devices may need to monitored by school personnel, but schools are not responsible for the implantation or replacement of such devices surgically. An example of this would be a cochlear implant.

The definition of *Child with a disability* is the term used for children ages 3-9 with a developmental delay now has been was changed to allow for the inclusion of Tourettes Syndrome.

IDEA 2004 recognized that all states must follow the National Instructional Materials Accessibility Standards which states that students who need materials in a certain form will get those at the same time their non-disabled peers receive their materials. Teacher recognition of this standard is important.

TEACHER STUDY GUIDE

Changes in Requirements for Evaluations

The clock/time allowance between the request for an initial evaluation and the determination if a disability is present may be requested has been changed to state the finding/determination must occur within 60 calendar days of the request. This is a significant change as previously it was interpreted to mean 60 school days. Parental consent is also required for evaluations and prior to the start of special education services.

No single assessment or measurement tool may now be used to determine special education qualification. Assessments and measurements used should be in *language and form* that will give the most accurate picture of the child's abilities.

IDEA 2004's recognized that there exists a disproportionate representation of minorities and bilingual students and that pre-service interventions that are *scientifically based on early reading programs, positive behavioral interventions and support, and early intervening services*) may prevent some of those children from needing special education services. This understanding has led to a child not being considered to have a disability if he/she has not had appropriate education in math or reading, nor shall a child be considered to have a disability if the reason for his/her delays is that English is a second language.

When determining a specific learning disability, the criteria may or may not use a discrepancy between *achievement and intellectual ability* but whether or not the child responds to scientific research-based intervention. In general, children who may not have been found eligible for special education (via testing) but are known to need services (via functioning, excluding lack of instruction) are still eligible for special education services. This change now allows input for evaluation to include state and local testing, classroom observation, academic achievement, and *related developmental needs*,

Changes in Requirements for IEPs

Individualized Education Plans (IEPS) continue to have multiple sections. One section, *present levels,* now addresses *academic achievement and functional performance.* Annual IEP goals must now address the same areas.

IEP goals should be aligned to state standards, thus short term objectives are not required on every IEP. Students with IEPs must not only participate in regular education programs to the full extent possible, they must show progress in those programs. This means that goals should be written to reflect academic progress.

For students who must participate in alternate assessment, there must be alignment to *alternate achievement standards*.
Significant change has been made in the definition of the IEP team as it now includes *not less than 1* teacher from each of the areas of special education and regular education be present.

OPTE

TEACHER STUDY GUIDE

IDEA 2004 recognized that the amount of required paperwork placed upon teachers of students with disabilities should be reduced if possible, for this reason a pilot program has been developed in which some states will participate using multi-year IEPs. Individual student inclusion in this program will require consent by both the school and the parent.

XAMonline, INC. 21 Orient Ave. Melrose, MA 02176

Toll Free number 800-301-4647

TO ORDER Fax 781-662-9268 OR www.XAMonline.com

CERTIFICATION EXAMINATION FOR OKLAHOMA EDUCATORS - CEOE - 2007

PO# Store/School:

Address 1:

Address 2 (Ship to other):
City, State Zip

Credit card number ____-____-____-____ expiration____

EMAIL _____

PHONE   FAX

13# ISBN 2007	TITLE	Qty	Retail	Total
978-1-58197-781-3	CEOE OSAT Advanced Mathematics Field 11			
978-1-58197-775-2	CEOE OSAT Art Sample Test Field 02			
978-1-58197-780-6	CEOE OSAT Biological Sciences Field 10			
978-1-58197-776-9	CEOE OSAT Chemistry Field 04			
978-1-58197-778-3	CEOE OSAT Earth Science Field 08			
978-1-58197-794-3	CEOE OSAT Elementary Education Fields 50-51			
978-1-58197-795-0	CEOE OSAT Elementary Education Fields 50-51 Sample Questions			
978-1-58197-777-6	CEOE OSAT English Field 07			
978-1-58197-779-0	CEOE OSAT Family and Consumer Sciences Field 09			
978-1-58197-786-8	CEOE OSAT French Sample Test Field 20			
978-1-58197-798-1	CEOE OGET Oklahoma General Education Test 074			
978-1-58197-792-9	CEOE OSAT Library-Media Specialist Field 38			
978-1-58197-787-5	CEOE OSAT Middle Level English Field 24			
978-1-58197-789-9	CEOE OSAT Middle Level Science Field 26			
978-1-58197-790-5	CEOE OSAT Middle Level Social Studies Field 27			
978-1-58197-788-2	CEOE OSAT Middle Level-Intermediate Mathematics Field 25			
978-1-58197-791-2	CEOE OSAT Mild Moderate Disabilities Field 29			
978-1-58197-782-0	CEOE OSAT Physical Education-Health-Safety Field 12			
978-1-58197-783-7	CEOE OSAT Physics Sample Test Field 14			
978-1-58197-793-6	CEOE OSAT Principal Common Core Field 44			
978-1-58197-796-7	CEOE OPTE Oklahoma Professional Teaching Examination Fields 75-76			
978-1-58197-784-4	CEOE OSAT Reading Specialist Field 15			
978-1-58197-785-1	CEOE OSAT Spanish Field 19			
978-1-58197-797-4	CEOE OSAT U.S. & World History Field 17			
			SUBTOTAL	
FOR PRODUCT PRICES GO TO WWW.XAMONLINE.COM			Ship	$8.25
			TOTAL	

www.ingramcontent.com/pod-product-compliance
Lightning Source LLC
Chambersburg PA
CBHW080540300426
44111CB00017B/2808